THE POWER OF LIFE

BEING A HUMAN BEING

By **Pesach Anderman**

Translation: Monique Goldwasser
Editing: Joan Handler
Production Manager: Avi Lifshits
OT Productions
Teomim publishing
www.ot-books.com

My Power of Life is dedicated to the younger generation, that it may learn and remember from whence we came and what we were, without a land of our own, how we lived and how we fought to retain our humanity.

Pesach Anderman

THE POWER OF LIFE

BEING A HUMAN BEING

The Rocky Mountains, October 1999

Table of Contents

PREFACE

When I turned 70, Hava, my wife, following her normal, determined nature, decided to throw me a birthday party.

Hava had hoped that this would be a surprise party, but since she had invited my sister Sali, her children and grandchildren from the U.S.A., and they had told me that they were coming to Israel in August, just around the date of my birthday, I began to suspect that something was going on behind my back. I discovered the secret approximately two weeks before the event… and deliberated as to how I should react to her "scheme". I was not comfortable with the idea of making a big deal of my birthday. I told her that this actually would be the first birthday that I would ever celebrate. I hadn't even had a chance to celebrate my *bar-mitzva*. Back then, in August 1942, these were not the most important things on my mind. I was busy, day and night, fleeing death that might be waiting for me at every turn. At that time, I was living from moment to moment, in constant fear, like a person who had lost his humanity and was forced to live like an animal, hunted by the Nazis and their gangs of fellow travelers. I was living on "borrowed time", on "probation", "fleetingly", because we could expect "*aktions*" at any time.

The party, as everything else my wife does, was flawlessly planned. Many people came from all over the world to take part in the occasion which she had organized in my honor. Heading the list were my daughter Amalia, her husband, Shmuel and my grandchildren Ophir and Yael, all of whom worked hard to make this a happy occasion. I sat at the table in silence for a long time, unable to utter a word. I was very moved. My joy was tinged with sadness because, as always during joyous occasions, the image of our beloved son, Ronny (*of blessed memory*), who was cut off in his prime, came to mind, and I felt the grief and sorrow that pursues us everywhere.

The congratulations and good wishes were, of course, very moving, but I felt detached, as if I was looking at the festivities from the sidelines. I sat looking at everyone, thinking to myself: why is it that only my sister and I survived the hell that we went through? Out of my father's and mother's entire families, only the two of us are left … and after we are gone, who will be around to tell the story of my father's family, the Andermans, and my mother's family, the Weistals, or the other relatives, the Bauer and Mandel families – no one is left. What do I know about them myself? What will I tell my grandchildren?

All I have left of that period are memories of the happy moments I spent with them as a child, and their impressive figures: I can still see them standing before me – handsome people, beautifully clothed – as if I had photographed them on some holiday or family celebration.

I think about them and about my parents – and even today, I find it difficult to understand why is it that none of them, particularly the adults, survived.

Seeing my family at the party, the close as well as the extended family, I finally decided, after many years of internal conflict, to begin putting the story of my life down on paper. I am dedicating this account to my sister Sali *(of blessed memory)*, to my brother Lonek Arieh *(of blessed memory)* and to my parents *(of blessed memory)*.

While writing this story, I sorely missed my sister Sali, who had shared in some of my experiences during the Holocaust, because she had been able to remember the past better than me, having been several years older than me. She had known the members of our family better than me and had better understood the events swirling around us when the war broke out.

I decided that I would tell my story without resorting to any "cosmetics", such as describing the landscape, or any "literary embellishments", without polemics or arguments. I shall attempt only to present facts and events that I experienced myself, relating them in the order in which they have been etched in my mind and in my soul.

Thousands of stories have already been recounted and written about the period of the Holocaust, and over the past fifty years or so, many studies have been made and published on the subject. My objective is that my story be able to add yet another small stone to the memorial monument.

It is very difficult for me to put my memories down on paper; it is distressing to recall this terrible period; it is horrifying to, once again, relive every event, every pursuit, every incident, and to bring back and put into words all of my experiences and the dangers through which I barely survived.

Today, I cannot even begin to understand from where I drew the strength for this. Where did I get the spiritual strength and courage to defy and refuse to give in to these murderers? To flee, again and again, determined not to get caught. How could I, a small and helpless child, face Germans and Ukrainians armed with rifles and knives, chasing me on horses, shooting in my direction, and yet, unable to catch me? Apparently the power of life is stronger than anything else in the world, because we, my sister and I were completely alone – I was only 11 years old and my sister, 17 year old, without any resources, without any help, constantly battling for survival. Escaping from operation after operation, "*aktion*" after "*aktion*".

No words can express our emotions at the time, all of our attention being solely focused on how to avoid falling into the hands of the murderers, how not to end up being led to the killing field like sheep to the slaughter.

I can't remember the exact dates of the "*aktions*"

anymore, but what I went through, my own experiences, are etched in my heart and in my mind forever – those, I shall never be able to forget.

The beautiful forests and landscapes I once knew are almost forgotten, vague shapes in the past. However, I can still recall the terrible hatred directed at the Jews as if it was yesterday.

Throughout history, many nations have vented their anger and hatred against the Jews by killing and subjugating them to indignities, even before the Nazi extermination machine was put into operation. Hatred for the Jews and anti-Semitism are deeply rooted in Europe's nations, and was evident even before the Inquisition, fueled by blood libels and virulent sermons in churches. However, without the support of the Ukrainians, the Poles, the Lithuanians, and populace in other European countries, the Germans would never have been able to carry out such mass extermination of the Jews.

This was also the case in Galicia, where I lived. I must, at this juncture, mention that there were, of course, a few Poles and Ukrainians who followed their conscience and who had good hearts. They helped Jews and some of the survivors owe their lives to them. I myself was the recipient of such humanity a few times. I am grateful to those (mostly women) who helped me, and yet – I cannot forget the others, the great majority, who helped the Germans in any number of ways.

Today, however, when leaders of those very countries

visit Israel, we sometimes hear them utter words of apology when standing in "Yad va-Shem", the memorial to the six million Jews slaughtered during the Holocaust, asking for forgiveness, but deep inside, I feel that this suggests a certain amount of hypocrisy, because their countrymen have, to this day, remained anti-Semites and still hate Jews, even countries where there are almost no traces of Jews left.

Even the Allies and the other countries who fought and resisted the Nazis cannot be completely absolved of these terrible crimes, because they did not lift a finger to save the Jews, even when the whole world was aware of what was being done to Jews in the extermination camps. What could have been easier than to bomb those camps? Their exact locations were known and at the least, this would have slowed down the pace of extermination, thereby allowing more Jews to survive. However, as we are well aware today, they did nothing.

And where were the leaders of American Jewry, then? Why did they not organize demonstrations in an effort to awaken public opinion and put pressure on President Roosevelt and the rest of the world's leaders to destroy all of the death camps?

I am often asked why the Jews did not band together and resist the Nazis and their cohorts? This question, in and of itself stems from an incorrect premise. First of all, quite a few Jews fought the Nazis as part of the Allied armies. Jews originating from what was, at the time, Palestine, also fought in the British army. We shall never forget the courage of the paratroopers who parachuted into occupied Europe, among them Hannah Senesh, in order to gather information and intelligence, and help those fighting against the tyranny of the Nazis.

There were even small pockets of organized resistance everywhere. Jewish partisans fought against the Nazis and their cohorts from the forests. Even our city, Buczacz, had isolated incidents of individual resistance, when people refused to be led to the slaughter like sheep, such as Yanek Anderman, my cousin who, when he was being taken with other Jews to be shot, broke out of line, grabbed a policeman's pistol and shot and killed a Ukrainian policeman. He was immediately caught, led to the city square, where his clothing was soaked with kerosene and set alight. His brother, Willi (*Zeev*), lives in Israel today.

It is, of course, clear that German ingenuity and planning was a great deterrent to the actual organization of large-scale resistance. It is difficult to imagine the psychological state in which the victims found themselves. The will of the Jews was broken by a process that consisted of a number of stages – at first, the Germans took their property and starved them, then they sent the men away to the work camps and only then did they begin to carry out the "*aktions*" and finally, the extermination, their "final solution". Thus, gradually, they were able to weaken the Jews emotionally and psychologically, until they broke. We must not forget that the Jews had always been an insignificant minority among the local, "goy" population. The local population was very instrumental in cooperating with the Nazis, whether playing an active or a passive role.

And then, even after everything that had happened in war torn Europe, the British shut the gates to the Land of Israel in the face of those Jews who had survived the camps and wanted to immigrate to Israel. I, myself, was a victim of this discrimination when, after the war, I came to Israel illegally and after being caught, was incarcerated by the British in the detention camp in Atlit.

Another tragedy which greatly saddens me, is the tragic death of those hundreds of young people, all Holocaust survivors, the exhausted remnants of large families which had been exterminated, who arrived in Israel in the midst of the War of Independence and who were sent directly to the front, only to be killed on the battlefield. Many of them did not even know Hebrew and most of them had not undergone any training in the use of weapons. I remember when some of these young new immigrants arrived at the prison camp in Jordan, having miraculously been captured rather than killed. They told us that they had been sent from the ship directly to the battlefront in Latrun, where bitter battles were being waged. They were later captured and tortured in the prison of the Old City before being transferred to our camp.

Many of the immigrant-soldiers fell at the front, some within the first few days of their arrival in Israel.

Some were buried in anonymous graves, their names unknown to this day. They had survived the battles of the Second World War, survived the concentration camps and had hoped to build a future in the Land of Israel, however, as luck would have it, they were not even given the opportunity to live as free men in their own country. *May their memory be blessed.*

This narrative, of course, was not meant to be a historical study. My objective, this preface, was to explain to the readers, in a nutshell and in simple words, the background to the story of my life, which will be related below.

I should like to direct a few words to the members of my dear and beloved family:

For many years, I debated with myself – should I lay out for you all of the chapters of "my life's story", even the most grueling ones? Will I be capable of describing what happened to me and to my family during the Holocaust? How shall I tell of the ways in which I survived this hell? Would you be able to understand the dangers, the terror, the despair, the loneliness and the pain? How can I explain how I was saved over and over again, after facing death so many times, escaping capture by the German beasts and their cohorts by the skin of my teeth?

In the past, I had decided that I would never tell my story because I did not want my children to grow up with such a heavy cloud over their heads. I was afraid that this might affect the course of their lives in some way. Therefore, I erected a kind of iron wall behind which I placed my past. I lived only in the present, with hope for the future.

However, today, having reached the age where one "closes" the circle of events making up one's life, and now that my grandchildren have grown up – I feel that it is my duty to tell my story. I feel that the youth of today is not conversant enough with the trials and tribulations experienced by the Jewish nation during its lengthy wanderings in the Diaspora. Therefore, I feel that it is our duty to tell our stories so that future generations will know and understand how we came to be here, in the hope that this may bring them to the correct conclusions with respect to our national future.

Just as we tell the story of the Exodus from Egypt at the Seder table during Pesach, we must remember, and remind others, of the horrors of the Holocaust. Anti-Semitism is still rampant in the world and there are even those who deny the Holocaust and make themselves heard.

The second part of the story, that of my life in Israel, provides me with the ultimate "revenge" and is related to the assumptions that we might have regarding our national future. The fact that we are living in a country of our own, and that we can now defend ourselves and ensure that we will have a free country of our own for the future generations gives me great satisfaction. We have not yet reached the end of our "struggle for existence" and the road to peace and serenity and living without tension is still long – but it is important to point out that what we have accomplished to date, what we have accomplished since the establishment of the State of Israel, in spite of the wars that we have had to fight, has never been matched in the history of any nation.

Things have not really changed – our enemies are still making every effort to destroy us and do us harm. There are large groups and organizations in the world that take every opportunity to criticize us and to spread anti-Semitic propaganda about us. They would like to see us weak and miserable. They have not yet understood that the Israeli is not the weak Jew they knew in the Diaspora, before the Holocaust. We are now secure in our belief that our way is just, and we shall continue fighting for our right to exist here, in our small country. No nation in the world yearns for peace more than we do. No army in the world is as humane as our army, and for that, we have already paid a heavy price, several times over.

I arrived in Israel before the establishment of the State. I took an active part in the Zionist–settlement enterprise by living on a kibbutz and working the land; I took an active part in the grueling battles for our independence; I served in the reserves; I contributed to the industrial development of the State of Israel; I raised a family. Today, I, Pesach Anderman, am a proud resident of Tel Aviv.

MY BUCZACZ –
The city of my birth

"This is the book of the history of Buczacz,
the Buczacz about which I write in my sorrow
and in my grief so that our sons who will come
after us, will know that our city was full of Torah and wisdom
and love and reverence and life and grace and kindness
and charity
until the ruinous abomination came, and
sin and the madness with it brought
with them destruction..."

S.Y. Agnon – "The City of the Fullness Thereof"

I was born in 1929 in Buczacz, Galicia, to David and Malka Anderman. At that time, long ago, the city of my birth was under Polish rule, but had known prosperity under the prior rulers, which were Austrian. This could be seen in the prevalent culture, of which there were a number of indications and most of all, in the use of German in conversations. The Jews, in particular, tended to use German when conversing.

Buczacz, which today is in the western part of the Ukraine, was located next to the western banks of the Strypa River, 55 kilometers from Tarnopol, the region's capital city, and approximately 100 kilometers from Lvov, the capital of Galicia during Austrian rule and the capital of Red Russia before Poland was divided for the first time in 1772.

Back then the city's population consisted of approximately 10,000 people (Jews, Ukrainians and Poles). The city was the center of small industry and boasted a rather large agricultural produce market.

The Jews of Buczacz concentrating mainly on producing spirits and exporting grain, pulses, beef, horses, chickens, eggs and pork bristles.

By the 20th century, there were approximately 7,000 Jews in Buczacz. Many Jews had left the city during the First World War, but most of them returned there after the war.

S.I. Agnon, the Nobel Laureate for Literature, wrote a thick book, The City of Fullness Thereof, which is about Buczacz, the city of his birth and where he spent his childhood: The book opens with the words: "My city is situated on mountains and hills and winds in and out of forests full of trees and bushes, and the Strypa River curls into the city and along the city, and water issues from streams and water canes and bushes and trees, and sweet water pours out of springs, and birds sit on trees and chirp from there."

The first mention of a Jewish settlement in Buczacz dates back to 1572 and since then Buczacz has witnessed the development of a strong and well rooted Jewish community. The Jews were merchants, plied their trade, buying and selling in fairs that took place in the city center and developed commercial ties with Turkey and other countries. Many of them were well-educated and well established.

However, the pride of the Jewish community centered upon its scholars. The Great Synagogue resounded with the voices of Yeshiva students studying Torah day and night. The city produced famous rabbis whose names were praised throughout the Ashkenaz communities. Buczacz was located in Galicia and the expression "Galicianer kopf" (Galicianer head/mind) referred to Jews whose minds were sharp and whose ability to dispute and debate aroused wonderment. It is no wonder that the majority of the community consisted of "mitnagdim", while the "hassidim" were an insignificant minority.

Buczacz was indeed a center of Torah education however, people such as Sigmund Freud, the father of psychology, came from there. He was born in Buczacz to a family bearing the name of Freide, but when the Austrians came in 1812, they "amended" people's names and the name Freide became Freud was used. Did he inherit also the quick "Galicianer" mind? Only God knows.

Various Zionist movements and almost all political trends were represented in Buczacz. Many members of these organizations and political inclinations immigrated to Israel from our city and became well-known and respected in many walks of life.

The Anderman family (which had apparently come from Germany) was considered to be among one of the oldest families in Buczacz and its surroundings. Due to economic difficulties and hard times, a large part of the family had emigrated to the United States in the twentieth century. In 1935, an organization was established in New York, dedicated to helping Jews who had arrived from Buczacz.

Most of the Buczacz Jewry lived in the city while a large part of the Christian population lived in the suburbs. Anti-Semitism has been rooted deeply in Ukrainians and Poles for many generations, with the focus of anti-Semitism being the accusation that the Jews had killed Jesus Christ, the Son of God. Christianity considered Jews collaborators with the devil. These were religious opinions that gave rise to the abasement of the Jews in many countries and cities: they were frequently expelled from their place of residence; attempts were made to force them to convert; blood libels were circulated and Jews massacred, at times, whole communities. The Ukrainians were blatant and loud in their expressions of hatred and would be at the forefront of pogroms against the Jews, particularly in the villages, where the Jews were always a minority. At times, these people would slaughter whole families, including babies, the old people and the women. In comparison, the Poles, who were more "cultured" despite the fact that they also hated the Jews to no lesser extent, knew, more or less, how to conceal this hatred.

My mother was born a Weistal and her family was related to the Bauer and Mandel families.

Contrary to the notorious stereotype that "all Jews are merchants", my mother's relatives were mostly involved in agriculture. I would often visit my aunts and uncles, all of whom lived in villages. I can still see them today, sitting in their beautiful carriages drawn by powerful horses, passing through the fields and the forests.

It is natural that the memories of my early childhood remain faint and somewhat blurred. In my mind's eye, I can see fragmented pictures; events blend into one another, a more recent incident often appearing before an earlier one; many details have been erased from my consciousness, if they were ever there; names have disappeared or have remained without a face to put them to ... Nevertheless, I shall put down on paper what happened to me, to the best of my ability.

Sometime after my fourth birthday, my father, David, fell ill with pneumonia. This was during a particularly harsh winter. The white snow was piled high before the house. My father was taken to the hospital and a few weeks later, died there from pneumonia. I was not aware of the full significance of his death and its exact consequence, that is, that I would never see him again. But everybody around me was sad, which made me sad as well.

During the funeral, I was told to remain behind, next to the gates of the cemetery, not allowed to enter, because I was a Cohen. According to Jewish religious laws, Cohens are not allowed to enter cemeteries so that they are not defiled and therefore prevented from serving God, particularly in the Temple. As a child, I did not fully understand the implications of all this (even today, I don't exactly understand it!). I felt humiliated. Why was I left standing outside? Why couldn't I also say goodbye to my father at his graveside? Had I done something bad?

This troubling memory has remained with me my whole life.

My mother, Malka, was left with three children: my sister Sali, my brother Arieh (*Lonek*) and myself, the youngest child. A great sorrow fell upon our family. The adored father, the beloved husband, the head of the family, the provider had left us. My mother was a beautiful woman, educated and gentle. She had dedicated herself to raising us and being a housewife. Father was assisted by a number of people who worked with him in the grain trade but mother had no idea whatsoever as to what went on in father's business. After his death, the business, of course, failed. I really don't know the details about that. My mother suddenly found herself alone in our house at the edge of the city, bearing the heavy burden of having to support a family. As soon as the "shiv'a" (the seven-day period of mourning) was over, when all of the mourners and comforters had returned to their normal lives and we were left alone with the grief and sorrow and all of the problems created by the loss of father, my mother decided to take matters into her hands.

My mother was a quiet person and bore the grief in the manner of a reserved, intelligent woman. This had a very definite effect upon us, making us restrained so that we did not show our grief in public, did not cry in public and saved our expressions of sorrow for inside our home. My sister and brother, who were older than me, pampered me and tried to make me feel better. Mother would sing sad songs to us.

After a while, my mother recovered and began dealing with the issue of supporting us. She took advantage of the good contacts we had always had with the farmers, most of whom had for years, come and gone in our home freely. She provided these farmers with items that they needed and in return, would receive foodstuffs from them and bring it home.

My sister was studying to be a teacher so that she could contribute her share to the family's support. My brother found some sort of work which he was able to do after school. Thus, from an economical point of view we managed, more or less. Maybe the most important thing in our lives was the fact that the atmosphere in our house was one of calm and serenity, and we all showed our love and consideration for each other. This was, for the most part, the result of my mother's demeanor.

My mother came from a well-established family and during the First World War, had studied at a university in Vienna. At that time, in the Ukraine, if a family had the means, it was customary for children to be sent to Vienna or Germany to be educated. This was a challenge and was considered to be prestigious. Despite the fact that anti-Semitism was evident even in Vienna, the atmosphere there was friendlier and more cordial than in the hostile Ukrainian environment.

My mother's broader education was suitable for leading a life of pampering and luxury, but had certainly not prepared her for dealing with problems involved in earning one's livelihood. Nevertheless, she succeeded in putting food on the table and we never lacked for anything.

During the winter, the situation was different – life was harsher and this is where I also came into the picture.

When I was eight years old the winter was especially severe. There was a snowstorm, it was very, very cold and the house was chilly and depressing. I mustered my courage, put on as many layers of clothing as I could find, took a bag and stick on end of which I had hammered a long nail and went outside. Once in a while, farmers would pass by with carts loaded with materials for heating. These were bricks made of packed clay that were over 100 years old and these could easily be pierced by a nail and strung onto my stick. I waited until I saw a cart that was loaded so heavily that the farmer could not see what has happening on the back of the cart. I would run behind the cart, jam the nail in a brick, causing it to fall on the ground, until I had collected a sufficient amount of clay bricks. Then I put them into the bag and took them home. The farmers had learned from bitter experience and every once in a while, they would flick the whip towards the back of the cart. More than once I received a very painful blow, but this did not discourage me. It was important to find a way to heat the house. The advantage of the clay bricks over other heating materials was that they were very flammable, did not produce smoke and did not emit poisonous gasses. Also a strong point, of course, was the fact that they were available.

During the winter, each time it snowed, the entrance to our home would be covered with a layer of new snow. We would stand outside for hours, in the freezing cold, grasping a shovel, clearing a narrow path to our house. This was hard work but was a good way to warm up the whole body. A thick layer of ice collected on the windowpanes, looking like flowers, as if drawn by someone. I remember how sorry I was when we occasionally removed the ice from the windows and destroyed nature's marvelous works of art.

In the winter, we would pass the time reading. My mother (*of blessed memory*) would read in German, my sister and brother, in Polish. I couldn't leave the house because of the cold. Schools were also closed, which didn't make me particularly unhappy.

When the weather changed and the sun came out and the wind died down, it was possible to go outside again and resume our daily routines.

In telling the story of my "bravery" regarding the clay, I seemed to have put the cart before the horse, so I shall go back in time.

One day, when I was five years old, I was looking out the window and saw a tall man, dressed in a Polish officer's uniform, coming up the path to the entrance of the house. I wondered why such a man was coming to our house? I was even a little bit afraid. And there he was, approaching the entrance to our house, followed by a youth carrying a huge package. When they entered the house, we children learned that this was my uncle Joseph, my mother's brother, who had come to visit us and brought us a cartful of foodstuffs. This was on a sled pulled by two huge horses and adorned with bells and decorations. I admired the sled and was very impressed by the uniform and officer's stripes. My mother was very happy, because the packages contained enough food to last the whole winter. He had brought us all sorts of good things: flour, eggs, homemade cheese and all kinds of fruit, the kind which would be able to last through the winter without becoming spoiled.

My uncle sat with us for hours and discussed the future of our family with my mother. He shared with us experiences he had had during his service as an officer in the Polish army. The thought that his family was left alone, exposed to dangers and tribulations because he was away from home was very difficult for him to endure.

He told us about the indications pointing to anti-Semitism in the Polish army, but since he was a high ranking officer – a Lieutenant-Colonel – he personally didn't have any problem in that direction.

From the moment that I laid eyes on Uncle Joseph, I was full of admiration for him. He was a man who commanded respect, admiration – he was powerfully built, tall and very handsome.

At one point, he placed me on his knee and told me stories about the family. I especially remember the story about my maternal grandfather – Aaron – and his exploits during the pogroms led by Petlora the Terrible, who came to our region with his Ukrainian soldiers, rioting and ravaging, butchering Jews and pillaging Jewish homes.

This was after the end of World War One – one day, this oppressor came with his Caucasian thugs to my grandfather's yard. My grandfather came out of the house towards him. He was strong and tall, with a long beard, and he faced the persecutor, looking him straight in the eye. All of a sudden, everything became quiet. Petlora looked at him. He saw standing before him a mountain of a man with a thick black beard, a Jew who was not afraid of him at all. Surprisingly and without any explanation, Petlora the Terrible ordered that nothing bad should befall this man and he should be protected from harm by others!

Maybe my grandfather reminded him of some colorful biblical character … maybe, when someone does not give in … at any rate, this time the family was spared the consequences of the pogrom. Other Jewish families were not so lucky.

My grandfather was beloved by all the farmers in the surrounding area. He was known for his kindness and his willingness to help his fellowman in times of need. He had a large estate as well as a store where he sold agricultural equipment and storage containers for grain and wheat, which were the crops that he exported. Other members of my mother's family also lived in the area, among them two sisters, whose families were involved in the commerce of seeds and agricultural equipment. These were well-to-do and respected families.

My father's family lived close to us. My grandfather Yehezkel and my grandmother Hanna lived next door to us. This was a large and spacious house. The large paintings hanging on the walls are still imbedded in my memory. These were portraits painted by different painters. Prominent among the portraits of my ancestors were some high-ranking military officers.

The family had apparently been living there for many generations because one could see many people in these portraits.

My grandfather was a religious man, very meticulous about his behavior and habits.

I would visit them every day and they would give me sweets and cookies. I loved playing in their yard with my cousins. I was particularly friendly with my cousin Adzio, who was a year younger than me. We would play a game similar to what is called baseball today. I would hit a wooden ball and run to marked spots as fast as I could. I always did well. Our Uncle Paisi and Aunt Aliza also lived nearby. My uncle was very tall, particularly compared to his wife, who was small. They spoke German. Her parents lived with them; their name was Stampler and they were apparently of German descent.

Neighboring farmers would often come to stop by to visit with my aunt and uncle. They would bring them cheese, fresh butter and fruits. The house was always full of people and laughter.

My father's sister, Aunt Rivka, lived on the row of single family homes. She and her husband Yisrael had two sons and a daughter. One of them, Shmuel, was my brother's age and they were very close.

In the summer, I would go visit my mother's relatives – particularly when the cherries had ripened. I would climb the trees and pick them. I would often come down from the tree completely black because in addition to red cherries, there were very black cherries. The garden also contained pear and apple trees – some would ripen in the summer and some in the fall. The apples that ripened in the fall were stored in the basement, well covered in straw, and would stay there the whole winter.

When I look back at that period, I remember these summers as the being the best days of my life. The weather was beautiful and the cherries, oh those cherries! To bite into that ripe fruit, the juice spurting out, never having enough!

The land around Buczacz was particularly fertile and all of the fruits tasted heavenly!

I would spend part of my summer with my Aunt Lola, who lived in a village called Trobochovcza. They would come to pick me up in a carriage. On the way, we would pass by a village whose name I can't recall, where we would rest in the home of relatives called

Bauer. This house was situated in a row of beautiful houses with large wooden verandas enclosed by railing with shapes carved into them, real works of art. When I reached my aunt's house, I was truly happy. The house was huge with many rooms, and servants. Cows, horses and other animals grazed and wandered around the house.

My aunt Lola loved me very much and spoiled me. I would go out in the nearby forest with them, riding on a horse. I inhaled deeply, enjoying the perfumed scent of the trees and feasted my eyes on the wild flowers, growing in a blaze of color. This truly was an earthly paradise. We would get off the horses, walk among the trees, picking berries and putting them in a large straw basket we had brought. After wandering for hours in the forest, gathering the berries, we would return home and it was then that the real celebration would begin. My aunt would take fresh cream, and pour it over the berries. We would eat this with slices of fresh homemade dark bread. What can I say – this is how I imagined that the food of the righteous in the next world would taste. Those were the best days I ever spent as a child.

My uncle was less interested in children. He was a very serious person and spent much of his time taking care of his business affairs.

For many years, my dreams consisted of recurrent images of those years and of members of my family. These were the nicest parts of my dreams. When I would wake up, I would return to the gray, stark reality that was to be such a significant part of my life for so many years. I don't know who lives there today or who pillaged all of my family's estates. I know that after the war, and even now, many people set out in search of their roots, but for the time being, I am still incapable of facing such a task emotionally.

There is one thing that has bothered me for many years – a question to which I have been unable to find a logical answer: what is the reason, the basis for this hatred of Jews that developed in the region in which I lived? When I accompanied my uncle during his visits with the farmers, I saw that they had the utmost respect for him and showed him much affection. Was this a pretense or was it part of normal neighbor relations? The Jews had always shown good will and been generous towards their farmer neighbors, whether it was by providing financial help or medical assistance or advice during an illness. My family had lived in the same place for many generations. To this day I can't understand how they could continue to live there, when there always appeared some new oppressor who would seduce the population against the Jews, and incite the "goyim" to participate in pogroms against the Jews, massacring and robbing them. At times, some of the Jews survived only because some goodhearted people hid them. There were a few, only a very few, Ukrainian farmers who were willing to risk their lives to provide a hiding place and refuge for their Jewish neighbors.

Another neighbor, who lived to our left, was the teacher. I remember his name – Kopler. I began going to his house from the time I was five years old to learn the "aleph-beit" (the alphabet), the Bible and to receive lessons on Judaism.

I remember that he had a daughter who was older than me. I don't know what happened to them, I can only guess.

My teacher was an impressive person, very tall, with a long beard, blue eyes, always wearing a long black coat and broad brimmed hat. My mother made sure that I went to his house every day to study. Since I was small, I really didn't feel very much like doing this because while I was studying, all of my friends were playing soccer or other games, and I didn't want to miss this. As I grew older, I learned to love the teacher and his lessons as well.

During the summer, the children used to go down to the Strypa River which flowed near our house, at the foot of the mountain. The climb back up the mountain was always difficult. The town of Buczacz had built a canal lined with concrete walls. At that point, the canal was only a few meters wide and the water was very deep. The canal led in the direction of the turbines belonging to the electricity company and the strong current of the water made them work. It was dangerous to bathe in the canal because of the strong current and therefore was not allowed. Only excellent swimmers swam there, because the current could draw a person into the station's turbines, killing him on the spot.

One day, I was standing at the edge of the canal with some friends. I must have been five years old. Someone suddenly came up behind me and pushed me into the water. I didn't know how to swim but I instinctively began beating the water with my hands and managed keep my head above water and not drown. The water was very cold because it had come down from the mountain, from the snow that had melted. That was my first swimming lesson, and I have been swimming ever since. Some time later, I was told that it had been a Polish boy who had pushed me into the water.

I began going to school when I turned six. There was a large Jewish community in the city, but our house was located at the edge of the city, so that only a few Jewish children were in a class that consisted mostly of Ukrainian and Polish children. These immediately made me feel that I was not welcome. All of a sudden, I had turned into a "zhid" and understood that I was a Jew, different, complete with all of the unpleasant significance of this concept. This was also the first time that I heard the expression "Jews, go to Palestine." The teachers did not do anything about the anti-Semitic exclamations aimed at me. They behaved as if they had not heard them. The children would lie in wait for me after school and shower me with stones. I usually gave back as good as I got and would start throwing stones back. I was quite a good shot because I was constantly practicing throwing stones at a variety of targets, such as trees or large rocks, and I had become quite good at it.

At home, no one became particularly excited when I told them about this. For them, anti-Semitism was a normal part of their lives. I should comment and point out that not all of the children were necessarily hostile. Some of them actually played with me and I even had a few Christian Polish friends. They came from homes that were more cultured and progressive. This was evident from their behavior. They were a small group and I never heard them utter a single anti-Semitic comment. We would also visit each other's homes and I felt comfortable in their homes. The friendship that I developed with them was a function of the existing reality, because with the exception of my cousins, there were not many Jewish children in our area. There were other Jewish children in my class but they lived far away, so we didn't have a chance to see each other very much after school.

My friends and I would meet and play soccer after school. The ball was made of pieces of material sewn together, and filled tight with pieces of material. We, of course, had to kick the ball very hard in order to make it fly and this would work, until the ball would fall into a puddle of water and would become soaked with muddy water. When this happened, the ball would become even heavier and if, heaven forbid, the ball hit anyone, he not only got dirty but would also receive quite a blow. This, however, never bothered us and we continued to play. We really liked to play "hide and go seek". We would play in the forest where it was always possible to find a tree behind which we could hide.

However, it should be remembered that these friends of mine, these Polish children, were very few indeed. Most of the children were infected with the concept of anti-Semitism which they had been taught along with their mothers' milk. There was no lack of unpleasant show of hatred for Jews directed at me as well. It goes without saying that these incidents were nothing compared to what was about to happen a few short years later.

The Russians Are Coming

We continued with our daily routine, in relative calm. One day everything changed. This was during the fateful summer of 1939. The whole world was shocked when on 23 August, Nazi Germany and communist USSR, which had been sworn enemies and were on the brink of war with each other, signed the Molotov-Ribbentrop Non-Aggression Pact. In a secret addendum to the Pact, both powers agreed to the division of Poland. The USSR agreed that the Nazis would take over the western part of Poland, in return for which, the eastern part would be annexed to the USSR.

Immediately thereafter, Hitler presented an ultimatum to Poland. Poland refused to accede to his demands and on September 1, 1939, Hitler's army invaded Poland.

Pursuant to this, England and France declared war on Germany and thus began World War Two. In the fall of 1939, Hitler subdued Poland. It took him all of two short weeks. The Germans called the attack on Poland a "blitzkrieg" (the lightning war). They swept through Poland with their columns before the Poles even had a chance to prepare themselves to defend their country. Most of the Polish army surrendered on September 19,1939 and the remainder was destroyed immediately thereafter.

This attack also succeeded, in part, because the Russians made it possible. The Germans were able to lull the Russians with the illusion that they only wanted Poland. However, in reality, the conquest of Poland was for them a springboard for an attack upon the USSR at a later date.

On September 17, 1939, USSR forces invaded Eastern Poland, as per the agreement with the Germans. This attack, without declaring war, was founded upon the claim that Poland had ceased to exist as a country and it was necessary to protect the "helpless" local Ukranians and Beylorussians.

The Russians took over our region, Galicia, without spilling any blood, without encountering any resistance on the part of the Poles.

I was approximately 10 years old at the time and not particularly interested in the ins and outs of international politics. One early morning, I awoke at dawn, along with all the residents of Buczacz, to the muffled sound of tank treads – the Russian army had begun entering our city. We were happy – we had been told that Jews weren't hated in Russia because the Communist regime absolutely forbad manifestations of anti-Semitism. I went outside quickly because I was very curious to see what Russians looked like. I had imagined them to be bear-like, very hairy, generous smiles on their faces. I ran alongside the advancing tanks in the street, very happy and excited, along with many of Buczacz's residents.

Suddenly, all singing stopped and the soldiers began coming out of the tanks, spreading out throughout the city. From afar, I could see a gathering of Russian soldiers. I came closer and heard a young girl crying. Her mother was standing next to her, weeping. The soldiers stood in line and one after the other, they raped the girl. The mother was sobbing, begging them to have pity. They paid no attention to her and continued to brutally rape the poor girl.

I was unable to bear this sight and, of course, I felt helpless, unable to do anything to help. After the first shock wore off, I rushed home. I was unable to tell my mother what had happened. I sat there quietly for several long minutes, trying to erase these terrible images that kept appearing before my eyes. I thought that the Russians were animals, without a drop of pity, with animal urges that are allowed to break out unfettered.

The Russians began to loot shops from the moment they entered the city. For some reason, what they wanted most of all were watches. When they saw someone in the street wearing a watch, they would immediately grab it for themselves. It was possible to see soldiers walking around wearing several watches on their wrist.

The Jews hoped that life would be calmer under the Communists. On the other hand, the Ukrainians and the Poles were afraid of the Russians, a reminder of past difficulties between the nations.

In view of the animalistic and barbaric behavior of

the Russian soldiers, all of the stories that been told that when the Russians arrive "things will improve" suddenly did not seem to be so realistic. It's true that the anti-Semitic cries in the schools stopped and lessons were "happier": many hours were devoted to public singing. We sang songs about the revolution, the soviet workers, Mother Russia, as well as folk songs (I heard many of these again later, when I immigrated to Israel); there was much dancing and I really liked that.

It was natural that our studies focused on the theory of Communism. I didn't quite understand what they were talking about and I wasn't even very interested in the battle between the social classes or in Marxist dialectics. The curriculum changed. We no longer studied the history of Poland or the writings of Polish authors. Instead, Russian authors replaced Polish writers, so that Mitskevitch was replaced by Pushkin, whose poetry I rather enjoyed reading at home. The schools were strictly supervised by the political officers of the Communist party.

It was not long before there was an acute lack of food under the new regime. In order to receive bread, we had to rise at three o'clock in the morning and stand in line in weather that was 20-30 degrees below zero. Sometimes, one would reach the counter only to find that there was no more bread. We found out that Russia lacked everything – food and clothing. It was no wonder that one couldn't find watches in shops.

Life in Buczacz under the communists was hard, and not only from an economic aspect. The illusion that they heralded the coming of the Messiah quickly dissipated. The regime picked on the Jews and the "rich". They confiscated their property and exiled some of them to Siberia. Only a few were able to survive there. The work camps there were notorious for their cruel treatment towards prisoners. Many were simply shot on a whim, others perished from hunger, some froze to death or simply died from exhaustion.

There was also no lack of manifestations of anti-Semitism, sometimes hidden behind the idealism of the class struggle and at times, direct and crude. There were no longer any illusions that Communism would free the Jews from hatred and persecution. Veteran communists grabbed all positions of power in the city. Some of them were even our relatives.

My brother was an outstanding student and after school, he was able to work part-time as a bookkeeper at the flourmill, so he was able to help my mother support the family. Our situation improved even more after my sister finished an accelerated course for teachers, became a teacher and began receiving a salary.

My brother became a member of the Komsomol, the communist youth group. He received a red kerchief and would occasionally go to the club – there too he was considered to be an outstanding pupil. I was very proud of him.

At the same time, a cousin of my mother's was appointed regional commander of the Communist Party, a very respectable position. However, the "contentment" did not last long: one day, we were told that he had been killed. The circumstances of his death were shrouded in mystery. No official explanations were received regarding how this had happened. All kinds of rumors flew as to the reason for his death. He had been in a position of power in the Communist Party – who would want to kill him? Some speculated that he had been killed by anti-Semitic Ukrainians who were opposed to the Communist regime. Others claimed that the murder had been committed by a jealous husband or a jilted lover. But it soon turned out (unequivocally but not officially) that the NKVD, the Russian espionage service, had "liquidated" him. This was Stalin's "purification" method – to do away with people who he thought had become too powerful and influential. In what way had our relative sinned? Beria, Stalin and possibly God were the only ones who knew.

We went to the funeral and for the first time (and the last time) I saw a "Communist" funeral— the deceased lay on the back of a truck that had been decorated with a red carpet and flying red flags. His face had been made up to look "natural". This was the first time I had ever seen a dead person transported in this way, in an open casket.

Representatives from the Party and the regime accompanied my mother's cousin on his final journey. This was a magnificent state funeral, during which soldiers fired salutes along the way. I was told that only "important" people were buried this way. All I could think was: "Don't do me any favors!"

We continued living under Russian rule. One day, my brother Lonek came home from school and told us that the principal had called him in, told him that he had been selected because he was an outstanding student and that he would be receiving a grant enabling him to study at the university in Lvov (Lemberg). He really was very intelligent. My mother was very happy that he had been offered such an opportunity, especially since he was only 15 years old, even though it was not easy for us to see him go. My brother went to Lvov and wrote to us once a week, letters full of awe about the beauty of the city, which had a large Jewish community, and the fact that he had found many friends there.

A few months later, he began sending us worried letters in which he told us that the Germans were creating Jewish ghettos in German-occupied Poland and that Jews were being transported to camps, where those that were incapable of working were being killed. This information seemed to be reliable since Lvov was situated on the border with the area of Poland that was occupied by the Germans. Similar rumors reached our city from other regions in German-occupied Poland. We preferred to ignore these rumors and did not want to have anything to do with them.

At the same time, relatives came from Germany, from Dresden, as refugees.

The family took them in and gave them shelter. The Andermans from Dresden confirmed the terrible rumors. They kept on telling us horror stories about what the Nazis were doing to the Jews, unable to stop repeating the stories incessantly. The Germans were sending the healthy men to work camps and the women, children and the elderly, to extermination camps. Only a few Jews, like them, had barely succeeded in escaping, leaving all of their property behind and paying huge sums of money in order to be spirited away to a safe place, such as our region.

Most of the Jewish populace in Buczacz did not quite believe, or did not want to believe these rumors. Some of the Jews were afraid and worried but only a very few of them decided to leave their homes and face the unknown. Apparently, most of them felt that they were safer in their own homes, and were afraid of leaving their safe haven and becoming refugees elsewhere.

On August 2, 1941, three million German soldiers invaded the USSR. Germany had violated the pact it had signed with the Russians. The attack was a complete surprise. Shocked and stunned, the Russian army retreated. Soldiers fled in shame. The Russian soldiers did not even make an attempt to fight the Germans. Columns of Russians fled, frightened. They looked wretched, no longer acting like a proud army that was ready to do battle for the motherland.

My brother Lonek came home in the midst of this confusion, coming all the way from Lvov on foot because all transport had been halted, and when he arrived, after having walked some 50 kilometers, his feet were very swollen and he looked disoriented, almost fainting. My mother and sister sat with him all night and he tried to convince my mother that we should all flee with him to Russia because we would all be in danger when the Germans arrived, which would be soon. They would undoubtedly kill all the Jews. My mother was not convinced by my brother's pleas and tried to persuade him not to go, to stay with us, because the journey was dangerous, and there were Ukrainian ruffians roaming the countryside. Despite our pleas, he was determined to leave Buczacz. At dawn, he joined my cousin Shmuel, and they fled to Russia.

Saying farewell to my brother was very difficult. My mother and sister wept. I fell asleep and so did not see him leave the house. To this day I am very perturbed that I did not part from him as I should have, because I never saw him again.

Later on, we found out that they had walked hundreds of kilometers, until they finally reached Moscow. We didn't hear from him for years. Finally, when the Russians liberated our region in 1944, we received a letter from him, from the front in Beylorussia. He wrote that he had enlisted in the army and had completed officers' training. He said that my cousin had reached a distant kolkhoz and had become ill there and died. My sister answered him with a long letter. She told him what the Germans had done to the Jews of Buczacz and the surroundings and how out of the whole family, only she and I had survived. We then received another letter from him telling us that the Russian army was preparing for a concerted attack against the Germans and that he would also be taking part in this. Apparently, the flame of revenge was strong and pushed him to fight, because he fell during this attack upon the Germans. This happened only a few months before the end of the war.

I missed my brother very much and thought of him often. He was a smart and intelligent person, gentle and good-hearted. The only thing I have left of him is a small photograph that had been part of his military identification papers that was sent to Buczacz after his death, along with a letter of commendation. We were not in the city any more but my cousin Willi took the letter and the certificate for us. He was able to save the photograph but the letter and military certificate were lost over the years and the subsequent troubles. He might even have been afraid to hold on to papers that could connect him to the Red Army.

When Willi immigrated to Israel, we met and he gave me my brother's photograph. To this day, I do not know where he is buried.

*My brother **Arieh**, z"l, before joining the Russian army, Moscow, 1943. Died in Belarus, March 1944.*

My Anger at God

The Russian retreat was chaotic. The Germans controlled the sky and their planes carried out untold bombing missions. A long retreating Russian train was bombed as it crossed a bridge. Some of the wagons fell into the gorge while some had already reached the other side of the bridge. I was not at home at the time. I suddenly saw many people running in the direction of the train. Without thinking, I joined the people running towards the train. At that time I was 11 years old, fast on my feet. The strong but pleasant smell of soap wafted up from the wagons. It turned out that some of the wagons contained toilet soap and washing liquid, products that were, at the time, very difficult to find. The crowd surged towards the booty, pushing and shoving. Despite the danger in which I found myself, I pushed my way through the crowd falling all over the booty. I found a small opening in one of the wagons. I quickly took off my shirt, tied the sleeves and threw bars of soap into them. I managed to collect approximately 50 bars of toilet soap and about 20 pieces of laundry soap. I ran home, taking care not to lose my precious package. When my mother saw me, she, of course, scolded me –how dare I go there without permission? How can I run around without a shirt?

Afterwards, we dug a small hole in the storeroom

and hid our treasure there. This "treasure hoard" of soap kept us going for a whole winter.

The Germans arrived in the city several days after my brother had left Buczacz, making a lot of noise with their tanks, motorcycles, trucks – all of these vehicles were full of soldiers with rifles with bayonets. They were able to advance very rapidly, because the Russians had not put up any resistance. We had been very surprised by this, because in school we had studied about the brave soldiers of the Red Army and had sung beautiful Russian marching songs. What we saw now were miserable, pitiful soldiers running for their lives, showing no signs of being ready or willing to do battle.

Once again, the Jews of Buczacz were filled with fear. There were rumors that the Ukrainians in the nearby villages had begun to attack Jews – they robbed them and in some places, several Jews were murdered. My mother forbade me to wander in the streets because "bad things could happen there." And so, I was shut in the house, something that was very difficult for me to do because, like all other children, I loved to run around and play outside. The days became endless and week after week passed in that manner. The only consolation came on Thursdays, when my mother would bake cakes for the Sabbath and the house would be filled with fragrant aromas. This small pleasure made our isolated lives a bit more bearable.

On the Sabbath, we would pray in the house, because we did not dare go to the synagogue.

The most difficult days were Sundays, because then

many young Ukrainians would come to town to go to church, and after the mass, they would get drunk. Every Sunday afternoon, we would regularly shut the shutters of the house and towards evening, shut off the lights of the front of the house, so that we would find ourselves completely in the dark. On their way home, the Ukrainians, walking in groups and gangs, all as drunk as lords, would walk arm in arm, singing Ukrainian songs at the top of their voices, and running wild in the streets. They would often throw rocks at houses belonging to Jews, breaking windows.

We would sit in the bedroom, which was at the rear of the house. As soon as we could hear the wild singing, we understood that they were nearing our home and we were very afraid, particularly since there was no man in the house that could protect us. We spent many a Sunday like this, luckily, without being harmed.

The atmosphere among the Jews was very tense because we did not know what awaited us in the future. The Ukrainian population and some of the Poles were happy that the Germans had arrived and received them with open arms, because they hated the Russians, particularly the communists. The Jews shut themselves up in their homes. They made sure they had enough produce and food at home so they wouldn't be caught out in the street, exposed to danger.

As soon as the Germans had entered Galicia, they began spreading their virulent brand of anti-Semitic propaganda, both in words and drawings. Jews were represented as blood-sucking leeches, as monsters and as enemies of the human race. They were blamed for all of the wars in the world and for taking advantage of the masses for filthy lucre. Posters were placed on the walls of Buczacz, showing the Jew Shylock, a twisted hunchback with a long nose, stretching his crooked hands in the direction of young innocent girls. This only fueled the hatred for Jews, a hatred which had already been burning for a long time.

Since we did not have enough food stored in our house, my mother decided to go to the village of Novostepsa. Only Ukrainians lived in this village. My mother knew some of them from the time that my late father had had commercial ties with them. The farmers treated her well, because she was a noble and impressive woman and always something to talk about with whoever she came into contact. My mother always went to those farmers that she knew would cooperate with her and wouldn't make problems. We received orders from the farmers for things they needed and they provided us with the foodstuffs we were lacking.

We would sell the farmers matches, flints for their lighters, soap that came from the "treasure" that I had taken from the train and sometimes, even kerosene for the lamps, because there wasn't any electricity any more. No money exchanged hands. It was all done through "barter". In return for the bars of soap we received flour, cheese, eggs and chickens. We kept some for our own use and sold the rest in the city. As I said before, most of the people were staying in their homes, not daring to go out, but once a week, we would go to the villages with our merchandise.

I was only 11 years old at the time but I helped, because I didn't want my mother to carry heavy things by herself. We walked across the fields, always staying on paths, with the corn stalks hiding us from the main road. We did this for obvious reasons – the Germans were using the main road and we didn't want them to see us.

It would often happen that we would reach a village and the farmers didn't have flour. Then, they would give us wheat and they would let us use the mill, which consisted of two large round stones with a handle on the side. This was very heavy and difficult to operate. I would stand across from my mother and we would turn the wheel together, grinding the wheat into flour. When we had finished grinding the wheat, we would divide the flour into two sacks and would go on our way, each carrying one sack. We sold part of the flour in the city and kept the rest for our own use.

We lived in this manner from day to day, with danger lurking at every turn. We learned to avoid danger as much as possible and tried not to build up our hopes too much. We managed to survive. The power of life, apparently, overcame all. We would return home from our forays, filling the storeroom with food for another two weeks. My sister did not go with us – she helped out with the house and spent most of her time reading books in Polish. Afterwards, she would tell us about what she had read. The three of us would sit in the kitchen for hours, my sister telling stories, my mother preparing food from what we had brought, humming German songs as she worked, songs she had learned while studying in Vienna.

Mother told us stories about Vienna. How beautiful and cultured was the city. But she did not like to talk about the Jews of Vienna. The Jews of Vienna had considered her, and those like her, the Jews who came from Poland and Russia, to be second-class Jews, in comparison to themselves, the elite of Vienna.

Life in town became more and more tense. More and more rumors were flying about what the Germans were doing to the Jews.

We, of course, had stopped going to school. Whenever I met a Jew in the street, he always looked depressed and worried. Many were beginning to be sorry that they had not fled to Russia.

The rumors that the Ukrainian population in the villages was murdering Jews were slowly and unfortunately being confirmed. Our aunt Lola informed us that my Uncle Josef and his whole family had been murdered. My uncle had been loved and respected by the farmers, and as I had explained above, had served as a high-ranking officer in the Polish army – but none of this was to do him any good on that fateful day, and in fact, may have even served to make the situation worse. Grandma Esther, the only one of the whole family that survived, had somehow managed to reach my aunt, who found her to be physically and emotionally ill, confused and disoriented. The severe trauma she had experienced had caused her to stop talking and my aunt was unable to get her to talk in order to find out how she had managed to survive. A neighbor from the village described the family's murder to my aunt. They even knew the name of the Ukrainian who had murdered the family, but there was no one to avenge their deaths.

My mother cried and mourned the tragedy that had hit our family. Most of her relatives were living in different villages – two sisters and a brother – and not one survived this hell on earth. I don't even have a photograph of the whole extended family. But I can still visualize my aunts' children, see how beautiful they were, how they loved and enjoyed life.

Jews began arriving in Buczacz in droves from the provinces because they felt safer among the Jews that were already living in the city. They refused to believe that their fate had already been sealed, it was just a matter of time.

One day, many SS soldiers arrived and announced that a ghetto would be erected in the city. With the help of Ukrainian units, they crowded all the Jews into an area that covered only two streets, thereby gaining complete control over the Jewish population of the city. The Germans closed these streets off with coils of barbed wire and surrounded the ghetto with guards. Anyone trying to escape was shot on the spot.

The Nazis formed a Jewish self-governing body, the "Judenrat", to which they attached a Jewish Police force. These two organizations were occasionally ordered to collect silver and gold and other items of value from the residents of the ghetto, which was then handed over to the Germans to help with the war effort. When the quotas that had been set were not met, the Germans retaliated by shooting certain respected members of the Jewish community. This served to put pressure on the Jewish leaders, who often had to make harsh decisions and take steps that were contrary to their conscience.

The members of the "Judenrat" were also responsible for providing a quota of Jews for the "*aktions*". Every "*aktion*" collected a group of Jews who were either sent to work camps or to extermination camps. Life in the ghetto was a matter of existing from chase to chase, from "*aktion*" to "*aktion*". The Nazis would surround the ghetto, shoot anyone trying to escape, assemble the people in the city center and then, transport them, like beasts, to their final destination. It was only some time later that we received details about the destinations. Sometimes, instead of transporting them, they would lead a group of Jews to the nearby forest, force them to dig large pits, stand them at the edge of the pits and shoot them so that they would fall, face down, into the pits they had just dug.

During every such "*aktion*", the Germans and the Ukrainians would search the houses, tearing down walls and ripping up floors in an effort to discover the Jews' hiding places. They also used dogs, who, using their sense of smell, were able to find Jews that were hiding, and they would then drag their victims brutally to the assembly points – from there, taking them to be killed. Very few persons tried to escape during the "*aktion*" and many Jews were shot to death, just on a soldier's whim.

We lived up a hill, at the end of a long street. We did not own this house. The former Jewish owners of our new home had apparently been killed. There were very few families left in the ghetto because many Jews were taken and deported during every "*aktion*". We were the only residents left in our whole building.

My mother fell ill. She had contracted typhus. The doctor diagnosed her illness but there was little that could really be done because no medicine was available. A typhus epidemic had broken out in the ghetto as a result of the deteriorated sanitation conditions, and it was claiming many victims. My mother was very weak and my sister cared for her to the best of her ability. She spent most of her time talking to her and stroking her hair. I would sit next to her bed, looking into her sad eyes. Despite her great suffering, no word of complaint passed her lips.

Sometimes, I would go out to get things that my sister asked me to get. I would bring back plants that my sister would boil in water to make a special tea for my mother which she drank without sugar, for there was none available. Despite her great pain and suffering, my mother would try to soothe us – "don't worry, everything will be all right, don't worry, everything will be all right."

I was in the room with my mother when she died. I immediately ran to call the "Hevre Kadishe" (the

Jewish burial society) to tell them while my sister remained in the house, and they took care of all the arrangements. It was a unusual for a person to die in his own bed rather than to have been murdered by the Nazis. I was unable to stop crying. All I could think was: "Now we have no one to care for us and no one to give us advice. We are truly alone in the world."

Once again, I found myself standing at the gate of the cemetery (burials were still taking place there) and history repeated itself all over again. I was not allowed to enter the cemetery because I was a Cohen. This was a very cruel thing to do – to leave a child outside the gates, while his mother is being buried inside. I cried bitterly, but it did not help – I was not permitted to enter the grounds of the cemetery. This trauma has hounded me my whole life. For years after that, I refrained from entering cemeteries, until my son, Ronny, was killed in an automobile accident in Europe. I was no longer willing to succumb to religious taboos and determinedly stood next to his open grave.

Since we all lived together in one room, it was inevitable that my sister and myself would also contract typhus. We lay in the sad, empty house, hungry and feeble from the illness, without any medical care. We asked someone to inform our Aunt Lola, who lived in a village near Buczacz. Our maternal grandmother was staying with her at the time and one day, she arrived at our apartment. She saw the state we were in and decided to take us somewhere else so that we could recover. We set out in the evening, walking slowly on either side of her, holding her hands, exhausted and weak.

While walking with my grandmother, I tried to get her to speak. I asked her – "where is Uncle Josef"? What happened? How did you get here? Why did you come here?" But she wouldn't answer. She looked at us with eyes filled with fear and dread. Grandmother had ceased to speak. As I related earlier, it was apparently a response to the traumatic shock she had experienced when my uncle and his family were massacred. My grandmother had been saved, but how? We were never able to find out, because she never spoke another word and when looking into her eyes, one could only find a reflection of fear, sadness and distress. Our grandmother's "noisy silence" was more eloquent than any words she could have used to tell us what had happened to her.

We walked with her for several kilometers until we had reached the outskirts of the city, communicating only with gestures. Her destination was an isolated house in which an old lady, a Pole, lived alone. My mother had known this Polish woman and would trade with her in the past. We hoped to find refuge with this goodhearted and compassionate woman. We were very afraid that we would end up dead, like our mother if she would not be willing to take us in and take care of us, because people were dying like flies from typhus.

When we reached the old lady's home, she agreed to hide us. My grandmother said goodbye and we never saw her again. I don't know what happened to her. At the time, she was living with my aunt, however this aunt did not survive the war either. The old Polish lady took care of us with devotion, as if we were her own grandchildren. She cooked special things for us, such as chicken soup. Luckily the house was isolated, located outside of the village, and people did not come there. For the first time in a long time, we felt safe.

As soon as we felt a little better and could stand, the good woman asked us to leave, because she was risking her own life by hiding Jews. We thanked her and since we had nowhere else to go, we returned to Buczacz, to the ghetto.

Once again, we had to come to terms with a new kind of existence. I could no longer go to the villages and we were constantly hungry. Then I had an idea. There was a large marketplace in the center of the town where the villagers would come every Thursday with their merchandise in order to sell their products and purchase whatever they needed. I decided to find a way of taking advantage of this economic opportunity. I had to take a chance so that we would not starve to death. I removed my yellow badge from my shirt, entered the marketplace and once again began "bartering" – offering flint stones for lighters, matches or cigarettes in return for food. I became quite an "expert" on the subject of flint stones. There were many frauds but because of the experience I had garnered, I had learned to differentiate between a good stone and a fake one that wouldn't produce a spark. The stones themselves looked almost identical, there was only a slight difference in color. I learned to differentiate between another type of deception: if there was too much color in butter, I knew it was not real butter; if a chicken's comb was white, I knew that it was sick.

Selling cigarettes was also lucrative and I became expert at identifying different types of tobacco by smell and color. I would buy cartons of empty cigarettes tubes with filters and I would cut up the tobacco leaves that I had bought into very thin pieces with a sharp knife. I would then fill the empty cigarette tubes with the cut tobacco and sell the cigarettes individually. Cigarettes were a luxury item because the farmers had been reduced to smoking cigarettes rolled in newspaper or thin paper, which was very expensive, making my cigarettes a real find. I kept all of my "merchandise" hidden away in special pockets sewn in the back of my coat.

There was always a German policeman, sometimes even two, wandering around the marketplace and it goes without saying that they were looking for Jews. They knew that Jews were working in the marketplace. Sometimes, I would come face to face with a German policeman. He would cry "Halt!" which was a rather common word, one which was often heard. I would stop, acting as if I had not understood what they wanted from me. The policeman would search the front pockets of my coat, which were, of course, empty. I had removed the yellow badge and there was nothing to indicate that I was Jewish. My nose, "symbol" of Jewish, looked completely Ukrainian. After having been accosted by soldiers, I would leave the marketplace right away. Other Jews trying to find some food were not as lucky, something in their behavior would give them away. The Germans would catch them, and the rest is history.

This bartering always took place under the shadow of death. However, in order to survive, we had no choice but to expose ourselves to danger. I was able to smell out danger and even if I didn't see or hear anything but only sensed danger approaching, I would take to my heels and run. Even then, as young as I was, I had already made up my mind that I would never meet death head on but that I would turn my back to it. If the worst happened, then at least I would not have to see the cruel faces of my murderers. If I fled, there was always a chance that I might be able to get away. The truth was that I was taking a big risk no matter what I did, but then the desire to survive can triumph over any fear, and if a person was not willing to take risks, he would not survive. I found ways of overcoming my fear and learned how to take chances, taking calculated risks, but always being careful because regardless of the situation in which we found ourselves, it could always be worse, and often was.

Almost alone in the ghetto, my sister and I scurried from house to house. None of our family was left and we had no one to lean on or to ask for advice. This existence gave us strength and we refused to succumb to despair and obstacles. We were not actively involved in the daily life of the ghetto, too preoccupied with our own battle for survival. Alone, young, without family, we survived, dependent only on rumors for finding out what was going on, never knowing when the next "*aktion*" was going to take place.

Despite the fact that I was only a little boy, without mother or father (I never liked the work "orphan") life had turned me into an independent person, responsible for all my actions. The situation and conditions in the city became harsher and harsher: there were murders, abuse, deportations. The few Jews left in Buczacz were frightened and desperate. The only person who gave me any hope was my teacher, Kopler, who had taught me Torah since the age of five. We had many "heart to heart" conversations and these helped me survive. He said to me: "You are 12 years old; this is the time for you to be learning everything that a Jewish youth must learn at the age of 13, the bar mitzva age." Then he would add, sadly, "I may not be here by then and there will be no one to teach you." This conversation moved me deeply. I saw myself, Pesach Anderman, as a kind of link in the Jewish chain that must not be broken – I had to live, I had to survive.

So many years have passed since then. So many cherished memories and images have been forgotten, but I shall always remember him. There, in the ghetto, he spoke quietly, almost whispering, every word penetrating my soul. In the dark, in the deserted and ruined house, he taught me the basic tenets of Judaism. Together we studied the Torah and he explained to me the values according to which a man must conduct his life. He constantly harped on the Ten Commandments and told me that I should fulfill the 613 mitzvot [religious precepts] to the best of my ability. At times, we would argue. I would ask him: "Where is God now? Why are they killing us? How have we sinned? Is it our fault that we were born Jews?"

Our conversations gave me strength, even when the answers did not satisfy me. It goes without saying that I found ways of repaying him. I would bring him food: bread, cheese, potatoes, and sometimes, fruit. He and his wife had nothing at home. It was touching to see them trying to hide their hunger and poverty.

During our conversations, he would say to me: "You will survive. You will to reach the land given to us by God, the land from which we were expelled two thousand years ago; you will survive – you have a good heart." At the beginning, I would reply that if I survived, I would flee far away, to the ends of the earth; I would not admit to being Jewish; I would live like all gentiles. I had suffered enough as a Jew! He would look at me and say: "You bear a distinctive mark, you will always be identified as a Jew, you cannot escape the fate of the Jews. You will not be able to hide from your identity, from yourself. Jewish suffering is in your soul."

When he spoke, his face shone and glowed. The hours I spent with him were for me the best hours. Time stood still. The rampant evil stopped outside of this snowed-in house and had no place inside. My teacher provided me with the only moments of peace that I experienced in those times and it all seemed surreal in the midst of the terrible reality unfolding outside of this sanctuary.

The "*aktions*" were renewed in the Spring of 1943: we heard shots at dawn and saw trucks carrying many SS soldiers enter the ghetto. As soon as they had arrived, they alighted from the trucks and began to run around, assembling the Jews of the ghetto. The SS German soldiers were helped by Ukrainians, who were worse than animals. Our house did not have a bunker and my sister and I, and a few other people who had been living in the house began running, trying to flee the city. We ran as fast and as far as we could and when we reached the Strypa River, we began crossing it on foot. The water was icy cold. It was a moonlit night. I looked back and shouted to my sister: "Look, they're chasing us." But she reassured me, saying that it was only the reflection of our own shadows in the water. After reaching the other bank of the river we entered the courtyard of the power station that had once been managed by Izo Reinish, my mother's cousin. There was an underground bunker under the floor of the stable, which was now empty of horses. One by one, we crawled into the deep pit, closed the cover over our heads and continued to crawl into the bunker itself. (Izo survived and after the war, immigrated to Israel where he raised a new family.)

We sat quietly all day, not moving. Towards evening, we suddenly heard noises and clatter – a German army unit had arrived, riding horse-drawn carts. They immediately put the horses into the stable above our heads. We were terrified that our presence would be discovered. There was a woman with a two year-old baby with us and every once in a while the child would begin to cry. When this happened, his mother would cover his mouth with a towel, almost suffocating him. We sat there frightened, hungry, for two days. Luckily, the Germans left after two days and we were able to breathe more easily. When darkness fell, we began leaving the bunker. But where could we go? Because we had no other options open to us, we went back to the city, to the ghetto.

When we reached the city, everything was quiet, almost pastoral. The street was almost deserted. I quickly ran to our house, to the room where I had been keeping two ducks that I had been fattening up for the Pesach Seder – one for us and one to sell. I had once learned the art of fattening poultry from farmers. I would lie on the ground, holding the goose tightly under my arm, grab its beak and open it with one hand. I had a small can of corn in the other hand and every time its beak was open, I would trickle a few kernels of corn down its throat. Before the war, it had been customary to fatten a duck before Pesach by feeding it corn kernels, thereby providing fat that would be kept in a jar for later use, as well as giving us meat for the holiday. Whoever was lucky enough to have a fattened duck could really have a feast. This may sound strange – but we were always hungry and our thoughts were constantly focused upon food... The door to the "fattening" room had been forced open, and the ducks, of course, were gone – not even a kernel of corn was left. The Germans had stolen the only thing I owned. I lay there on the floor, in the dark, hungry, wondering – how could I get something to eat, something to drink?

The next day, I went to see what had happened to my beloved teacher. As I neared his house, I became very anxious: could he have survived? The whole house was open, everything strewn about on the floor and the teacher and his wife were gone. I burst into tears and shouted: "God, where are you? Who will I speak to? Who will teach me? Did he deserve this, this man who never harmed another person in his whole life, whose faith in You was his whole life? God, why didn't you help him?" I was very depressed and very angry with God.

The Little Matchgirl

Somehow, we resumed our grueling daily routine. Only a few hundred Jews were left in the city. Our house was empty. There was nothing there to distract us from the horror of the reality around us. There certainly were no games. My sister spent her spare time, of which there was much, mainly reading. I read less. Mostly, we talked.

On Thursday, I went to the market as usual, going about my business, because we had to survive. In the market, I listened to stories about how they had taken the Jews to the "Pedor" to be killed. The "Pedor" was a beautiful mountain where young people would walk on Saturdays and holidays. The Germans had ordered groups of Jews to dig a large pit, to get undressed, and then they mowed them down with a machine gun. Rows upon rows of naked Jews fell into the pit. The farmers at the marketplace also told stories about murders, abuse, torture and other atrocities – it was hard to comprehend how people were capable of committing such barbaric acts. I listened to these stories in a daze, as if they had become a routine part of our lives.

At that time it was still possible to "wander around" a bit. While wandering through the marketplace, trying to sell something to the farmers, I suddenly heard someone crying bitterly at the end of the square. I ran to the other corner and saw a little girl called Dvora, shouting and crying. I asked her: "What happened to you?" She pointed to a Ukrainian boy standing on the side and said that he had grabbed the few remaining boxes of matches that she had left to sell. Without thinking of the risk involved, I grabbed a stick, ran to him, and shouting at him, grabbed the carton of matches out of his hands and returned it to the little girl, who thanked me tearfully.

The Ukrainian did not react because many people were present and he was confused by the attention that his despicable act had attracted.

[Sixty years have passed, and one day, during a memorial service for the martyrs of our city that was being held in the Holon cemetery, this same Dvora, formerly Grinfeld and now Diamant, came up to me and embraced me.]

On my way home from the market, I would often run into people desperately looking for a morsel of food. I would give them part of what I had in my sack. My daring and talent for disregarding any danger that might befall up because of my actions when I left the ghetto at least resulted in some measure of benefit for my sister and myself – food. During that period, we were never hungry.

I was aware of the risks that I was taking and the dangers lurking around every corner. I always took precautions not to run into a German or Ukrainian policeman, because the price for this could be very dear – my life. I was always glancing everywhere, always alert, my instincts very sharp. I would try to complete my "bartering" activities as soon as possible. I would set a "price" for every item I had and was always able to receive the goods that I had counted on taking home. I would look at a woman sitting with the goods and approach her to exchange merchandise. I refrained from approaching old men or young boys, because one could never know what kind of evil might lurk there. I learned to get to judge people by the look in their eyes and with the first words I would exchange with them. I must emphasize that few youths my age dared to do what I did. However, for me, this was a way of dealing with life. In fact, because of the circumstances in which we were living, the issue of "life or death" became something which was completely natural, a kind of habit, a way of life.

A new neighbor, another one of those who had survived the last "*aktion*" came to live in the same house. She was, apparently, a wealthy woman. She would pay someone to bring her food so that she would not have to leave her rooms. One day, I said to her: "Why don't you buy from me? I'll sell you food for less." And thus, I had another client. I became one of her favorite people and she would get great pleasure in stroking my head when she would thank me for my help.

The streets of the ghetto were almost empty, only very few people daring to leave their homes and go out. Most shut themselves up in their homes. Early in the morning, I would see groups of men going out to work for the Germans. When they called for men and youths to present themselves for work, I would never answer the call, because I was afraid that this was only a pretext and that they didn't really intend to take people for work, but rather, to take them to be shot.

When I wandered around the ghetto I would meet people who were terrified and the looks of utter despair and defeat in their eyes left me chilled to the bone. However, the very fact that I was living in such an environment, in an atmosphere of uncertainty regarding my very future, in an atmosphere of despair and misery actually gave me strength and reinforced my resolve to survive, and perhaps to be able, one day, to see better days.

Our "routine" continued thus for another month. My sister would sit and knit sweaters from the sparse wool that was left. The house we lived in was empty but for us. We were alone; no one came to visit us. This was somber atmosphere, one that was difficult to describe.

One day, at dawn, we once again hear the sound of vehicles and SS commandos arriving to carry out the last "*aktion*" in the ghetto. My sister and I jumped out of the window right away and ran towards the outskirts of the city. We hid in the fields, among the wheat sheaves that had been harvested and arranged in piles of threes. We hid in a hollow space formed by the sheaves. This field was large and there were many such piles of sheaves. We sat and waited for the "storm" to pass. We returned to the ghetto two days later, as we had done before, over and over again, because we had no where else to go. For the thousandth time, we saw the horrible tableaus of bodies and blood in the streets. The atmosphere in the ghetto was one of total despair. Only very few had survived this last "*aktion*". A few days later, there was a rumor that the Germans had decided to demolish the Buczacz Ghetto. Whoever remained would be transferred to the Tluste Ghetto, 40 kilometers away from Buczacz. The city of Buczacz was to be declared "Judenrein" - "Free of Jews" - and heavy punishments would be meted out to those who hid Jews.

In any case, no one in the city would dare to help the Jews, either because of anti-Semitism or because this would indeed put the person in mortal danger. The neighbors would be aware of this immediately and probably inform the Germans in return for some sort of reward. In the outlying farms, it was a different story. There, the houses were more isolated and distant from each other, and it was more difficult to discover that someone was being hidden, thereby lessening the risk for those persons hiding Jews. There were some farmers who agreed to hide Jews – whether because of friendly relationships in the past, or in return for money, or simply because they were brave and good people – Righteous Gentiles.

One day before the Jews were to be transported from the ghetto, my uncle Paul, my father's brother, came to the city with his wife, their three children and his wife's parents. They had been hiding with a Polish farmer who had become afraid and was unwilling to continue hiding them.

The morning arrived when the deportation was to be carried out and we began to make plans to leave the Buczacz Ghetto. My uncle rented a cart and put his wife and children on it and we walked next to them the whole day. In the evening, we reached the city of Tluste, which lay between Buczacz and Tchortekov. We entered the ghetto. We found some empty space on the ground floor of an empty house in the ghetto. My uncle's eldest child, Arieh, who was nicknamed Adzio, was a year younger than me. We became friends and were always together during those days. My aunt's parents spoke only German to each other but I don't know where they had come from originally. We settled in but it all seemed so strange and alien, I didn't know where to start or what to do with myself. Very soon, a week after our arrival, just when we had begun getting used to the place, we heard shots and noises at dawn and knew that there was an "*aktion*". Our aunt shouted at us to jump out of the back window of the house – "children, save yourselves, run," she screamed. My sister, my cousin and I jumped out of the window and each of us ran in a different direction, away from the city, towards the fields. This was the first time that my sister and I did not escape together. I ran towards some village and entered the first farm that I saw. I climbed up into to the barn and hid among the straw bales. There was a large pile of sheaves that reached up to the roof, which was also made of straw, and when I moved some of the straw aside, I was able to make a small hole and see what was going on below. Suddenly, I heard shouting and saw that Ukrainians had arrived with the S.S. They assembled everyone in sight. They collected some 40 adults and children, as well as a pregnant young woman. Suddenly, the commander of the Ukrainian unit arrived and shouted: "Do not shoot them! It's a shame to waste bullets!" There was sudden quiet. The people looked at him. Without making a sound, he took a pitchfork and killed them all himself. The pregnant woman was left for last. He first pierced her belly and then stabbed her in the other parts of her body. I shall never, as long as I live, be able to forget this appalling sight. Even now as I sit and write these words, I feel a tremor run through my body. But then, at the time, I could not allow myself the luxury of to dwell on the horrifying experience of witnessing this horrible picture. I had to dull my senses somewhat in order to be able to remain resolute, to continue to fight for survival, to go on, even if there was no shred of hope.

I remained hidden behind the bales of hay, eating seeds of grain as my only sustenance the whole time I was there. Two days later, when darkness fell, I came down the ladder very quietly and began walking in the direction of the city. When I reached "our" house, I was confronted with a shocking sight. The house was empty. Here and there were strewn objects and clothing belonging to my aunt and uncle, all spotted with blood. There was no sound. The apartment was absolutely silent. I sat silently in a corner, alone, hunched up like a fetus, pictures of my uncle and aunt flitting through my mind. A few hours later, my sister arrived at the apartment, followed by my cousin, both having miraculously survived. Adzio wept bitterly. We did not know how to comfort him and our attempts to do so were in vain. Just two days ago he had been with his family and now, he found himself alone in the world. What could we say to him? Once in a while we caressed him, and we wept with him.

Each of us told the others where we had been and how we had hid. My sister and cousin had seen how the Germans and the Ukrainians had caught and slaughtered Jews.

A few days later, Adzio decided that he would go to Tchortkov. We had an aunt living there, our fathers' sister, to whom he was very attached and he had decided he wanted to live with her. When we met up with him again a few months later, he told us that he had been terribly disappointed when he had reached the aunt's house. The house was empty. Apparently, the aunt had been killed during one of the "*aktions*". Since he didn't know anybody else there, he decided to travel back to the vicinity of Buczacz, where he knew a few villagers who had had business contacts with his father. Our cousin hoped that they would give him shelter. We didn't hear from him after that and our ways parted. The only member of Adzio's family who survived and reached Israel was Yitzhak, the son of our aunt from

Tchortkov. His road to Israel was one of persecutions and troubles, but he survived.

My sister and I stayed in Tluste, in the small ghetto, but rumors floated back from the local "Judenrat" that the Germans had also decided to liquidate the Tluste Ghetto. There were several work camps in the vicinity. Under the circumstances, my sister and I decided that the best thing for us would be to go to such a camp. My sister was taking care of me because I was still young, only twelve and a half, and she was worried: "How will you be able to survive the hard labor? Stronger men than you have not survived." I convinced her that I was not so weak and would be able to do what they told me to do. She was afraid, as usual, but I explained to her that if we did not go to the work camp, we would probably be executed. That evening, we approached the leaders of the ghetto and asked to be transferred to the work camp. They looked at us with pity, shook their heads, but did not try to dissuade us. The next day, we were taken to the work camp.

I was placed in the men's huts, and my sister, in the women's huts. Every hut held about 50 people. The work supervisor there was a cruel Ukrainian who would cold-bloodedly murder anyone looking at him "cross-eyed". He would do so by beating his victim with heavy blows from a bludgeon that he always carried with him. I tried to stay away from him. The camp commander was a very tall man, a Pole from Silesia. He had a mistress, a beautiful Jewess, who lived with him. He would ride a huge horse, holding a leather whip that was tipped with a steel ball. We would go out to work every morning, baling wheat, which would be tied with straw that had been woven several times until it formed a rope. The work pace was murderous. We would all start out at the same time, in a long line, and whenever someone fell behind, the commander would come close to him on the horse and beat him until he drew blood. There was very little food – only soup made out of dead horse that could be smelled from afar, and one small slice of bread. Despite my hunger I preferred to take only bread and water. We were also put to work in the rubber plantations, for what was called the "German war effort". We began working at dawn and our day would end at nightfall. Sometimes, they would carry out "selections". They would select the strong and kill the weak, the ones that could no longer work and were therefore useless.

Everyday, life in the camp became more difficult and more precarious. We heard that SS units, accompanied by Ukrainian policemen, would sometimes arrive in the work camp in Holovencitsa, only a few kilometers from us. The Germans and their cohorts would encircle the camp, assemble several hundred people, lead them to the forest and shoot them while they were standing at the edge of large pits that had been prepared in advance. We were afraid that our turn would come very soon. We heard no news about what was happening at the front. Were the Germans beginning to retreat? Had the Russians begun their counter-attack yet? What were the Allies doing? We continued to work in the fields from morning to night, not knowing what the next day would bring. It was very difficult. The people were exhausted and many suffered from different sicknesses.

At night, I would dream that they were coming to take us to the forest, to the killing field. I tried to hold on to some thread of hope. I discussed my thoughts with my sister but she always tried to temper my enthusiasm for ideas I presented, and would calmly say: "It's more dangerous out there" over and over again.

I heard rumors that there were Russian partisans in the forests. They would mount guerilla operations against the Germans from there and even managed to kill some of them. I tried to find out how we could reach them, but no one knew their exact location. Looking back, I was lucky that I couldn't reach them. From what I know today, they did not want Jews joining them, certainly not a Jewish boy. They did not especially like Jews. There were also Jewish partisans in the forests who wanted to help the non-Jewish partisans fight the Nazis but they were not accepted either. They refused to let the Jews fight with them. If they let Jews take part in the battle at all, it was as separate units. They would send them out to carry out the most dangerous missions, and many Jews were killed during these operations. A small part of the farm population helped the partisans (the non-Jews), providing them with food and information about the German army. The majority, however, cooperated with the Germans and whenever they had information as to the location of partisans, they would inform the Germans. As a result, the Nazis would find the partisans and kill them. Then, other partisans would come to the farms and murder the farmers in revenge. They were not always careful to differentiate between informers and innocent people. They would simple come and shoot. Without any discussion, without any trial. Human life was indeed cheap at the time.

I had been in the camp for several weeks when one day, again at dawn, we heard the noise of trucks and a disturbance coming from the direction of the camp gate. Suddenly there were shots. Having had previous experience in escaping, I ran to my sister's hut and together, we climbed through the camp's barbed wire and ran. It was still dark and we ran very fast. I don't know where we found the strength for this. We met some people along the way and joined them. We reached a hill in the forest, climbed to the top of the hill and sat down under a large tree. In the meantime, other escapees joined us and then we were approximately 14 persons, huddled under the huge tree that spread it's great branches over us – so that we felt as if we were in a kind of shelter that nature had prepared for us and which would keep us from all harm. Below us, at the foot of the hill, we could see a large wheat field, perhaps three kilometers long. It rained heavily during the night and we all became soaked to the bone. In the morning, with the sunrise, we took off our wet clothes and hung them on the branches of the tree to dry.

Around ten in the morning, we suddenly heard shots and a few Ukrainians wearing SS uniforms appeared on horseback. They surrounded us and began killing people everywhere. My sister and I ran in the direction of the wheat field, towards the open space. I was almost in shock, but as I was running, I shouted to my sister: "Look, they're coming toward us!" and my sister yelled back, "follow me!" She turned right and a few hundred meters farther we lay down in a small ditch, clinging to the ground, trying to be invisible. When we looked over the edge, we saw the Ukrainians galloping on their horses, looking for us. I shall never understand why they didn't find us. I could see them but they couldn't see us. If they had only glanced in our direction things would have turned out completely differently! We could hear the sound of shots in the background. An hour later, everything became very, very quiet. Deadly quiet. We continued to press ourselves to the ground until dark, without moving. When night fell, we arose. "I'm thirsty", I said to my sister. "Lick the dew off the leaves, or urinate and drink the urine", she replied. The night was cold, and I was shivering - my upper body was bare, because I had hung my shirt on the tree to dry. I shall never understand why I didn't catch pneumonia then, I was so cold.

The sun came out in full splendor and began warming our frozen bodies, but we continued to lie in the ditch because we were afraid that farmers might be wandering around the huge tree, under which 12 Jews had been murdered. Usually, after incidents such as these, the farmers would come and look for booty. We were familiar with this from all of the previous "*aktions*". We peered from afar to see if there was any movement around and continued to lie there so that we wouldn't be discovered. The only thing we could see were the tall fir trees at the entrance to the large forest, but we did not dare to approach it in daylight. The wheat stalks were wet from the strong rain that had fallen and I licked the drops of water that had not evaporated in the sunshine. I told my sister that we should go back to the tree which had sheltered us – maybe we would find my shirt and then I could be warmer when evening came. She convinced me that it would be better for us to wait because the danger had not yet passed.

The day dragged on, and I waited impatiently for it to become dark so that we could get up and stretch ourselves. At nightfall, we slowly and carefully began to walk towards the tree. To my great joy, I found my shirt on one of the branches. It had dried in the little bit of sun that had managed to penetrate through the branches. I hastened to put it on and felt a little warmer.

We saw bloodstains on the tree trunk – the only signs of what had happened there. The images of the people with whom I had been only yesterday, passed before my eyes. Now there was no sign to show that they had even been there, except for the bloodstains on the tree and on the ground. Many thoughts passed through my head. Was our dead mother praying and looking out for us? Keeping us safe? Or was it simply a miracle that we had survived? Maybe the fact that we were together, supporting one another, gave us the strength to continue and deal with our cruel fate.

The forest was huge. The trees thrust up very high and the total silence was soothing, particularly after the storm that we had been through during the past two days. Here and there we could hear the gay chirping of birds that, once again, had begun flying around after the rain had stopped.

We discussed what we should do, where we should go. We decided that we had no choice but to return to the camp. The very thought of reentering that place, where there was no hope, did not exactly make us jump for joy. We knew that many of the camp's inhabitants had already been killed, but the Nazis always made sure that they brought more people that came so that there would be enough workers work for them in the fields. Once again I saw Jews with bowed heads, eyes lowered, dragging their aching bones to the parade grounds to be counted before going out to work.

At nightfall, my sister and I began walking in the direction of the camp. We simply had nowhere else to go. We were in strange surroundings, where there was no one to whom we could turn to shelter us from the dangers lurking at every turn.

We each sneaked into our own hut. I saw that very few people had survived the last massacre. They told me what had happened. The Ukrainian murderers had gathered all of the people onto the parade grounds and led them to a nearby ravine. Once there, they mowed them down with gunfire, with the exception of a handful of people who were told to cover the bodies with dirt.

In the morning, we again arose to go to work. The path we took was lined with very tall trees on both sides. This was a very beautiful avenue, which, at one time, must have been very pleasant to walk through.

Next to the tree-lined avenue were a few isolated farmers' homes. A number of people were busy hanging tobacco leaves to dry. A young girl of about 12 was standing in the doorway of one of the houses. She looked at me. I asked her to prepare a slice of bread for me for the next day. She nodded her head and I took that as a sign that she had agreed to do that.

The next morning, very excited, I waited for the moment that I would meet her again. When I reached the gate of her house, the girl wasn't there. I was terribly disappointed but then I saw, on the ground, something wrapped in paper. I looked around to see if anyone was taking any notice of me, bent down quickly, picked up the little package, where I found a large and delicious slice of bread. I quickly hid it under my shirt and ran to find my sister. We shared the marvelous treasure that had fallen into my hands. This continued for a few days. Usually, she would leave a package and I would collect it. After a few days, I again saw the girl standing at the gate. She was very pretty, with blue eyes, a long braid and the face of an angel. I whispered to her that I wanted to work in her farm, hanging tobacco leaves. She said that she would ask her parents.

The next day, when I met her, the girl said that her

parents had agreed to employ me and I could come to them whenever I wanted to.

I told my sister, who, naturally, reacted with fear and tried to explain to me the risks that this involved. She claimed that I might get caught trying to escape from the camp, that one should never trust strange farmers, that I had been lured by a beautiful "shikse's" manners and even if everything was on the up and up, it would be easier to catch me that way. However, I was not willing to give up my decision to try my luck working outside the camp. I had to admit that it was not only considerations of survival that were the driving force and that my sister wasn't completely wrong when she said that the girl had influenced my decision.

In the evening, when I returned to the camp, I met a boy my age whose name was Abraham Shumer. [He lives in Ashkelon today and deals in agriculture.] I suggested that we run away early in the morning and go to the farmers and work for them drying their tobacco. At least that way we would get a loaf of bread. He agreed enthusiastically. In the early morning, we slipped out of the camp and reached the farmer's yard. I saw the girl there and she smiled at me, a smile that seemed to come from the heart. We approached her parents and asked for work in return for a loaf of bread. To our delight, they agreed. They showed us how to sort the leaves, string them and hang them up to dry. We began to work in earnest. Two hours later, we suddenly heard the sound of a horse's hooves. We turned around and found ourselves facing the camp commander. He shouted at the farmer, ordering him to bind our hands together immediately. He used very thin, very strong, linen rope, and every movement cut into our hands. The camp commander began to make us run towards the field. On the way, he beat us mercilessly with the tipped leather whip. Every blow left a mark on our back and on our head. When one of us fell, he beat him until he rose. Sometimes we felt that the horse's huge feet were about to crush us. Bleeding from cuts all over our bodies we reached the field where the others were working. He placed us at the beginning of the large field in which we were to work and we had to catch up to the other workers, who had already advanced quite a distance. We worked at a murderous pace, being constantly whipped to make us work faster. My sister saw what was happening and ran towards me. She begged the commander to be allowed to help me so that I could catch up, but he began beating her as well and she was forced to return to her place in the field. That was a terribly difficult day for me. After work, I returned to the camp, beaten and sore, covered with blood. I was afraid that they would take their revenge on me that day and take my life.

I decided that it was imperative that I get away from the camp and find another place to hide before the Gestapo came for me. I told my sister what I was planning to do. As usual, she begged me not to, crying that I was risking my life, but I was adamant. I set a time that I would meet her two days later at night, two kilometers away from the camp, where the forest began to get denser. I drew a plan of the exact place for her in the air.

How did I manage to get out of the camp each time? First I would stroll near the fence and look for a break of some kind in the fence, through which I could crawl and get out. I did not have any tools to cut the wires. But the camp was located in the middle of a large field and of course, fields have clumps of dirt. There was a ditch covered with dirt under the barbed wire. I crawled out of the camp through there. Very few people fled the camp. The people were already worn out, they had already come to terms with their fate and they did not have any more strength to fight for survival. They were weak and bewildered, and most of them were completely apathetic. In contrast, for some reason, I was very alert, aware of my surroundings and determined to survive.

Within a short time, without hesitation, I crawled under the fence and walked a few kilometers, until I reached the courtyard of a strange farmer. I had no choice. Despite the fact that there was a possibility that he might hand me over to the Nazis, I "took a chance", entered his farm and asked him to let me work for him in return for food and a place to sleep. This was a turning point my life, and as it turned out later, for my sister as well.

To my surprise and joy, the farmer agreed to take me in. I later found out that he was the deputy head of the local council. I asked him to find a hiding place for my sister as well. I said that she could knit very well. The farmer's wife heard me and suggested that she ask her sister if she had room for my sister. Her sister agreed to give my sister work and let her stay in the barn. Thus, even before I went to meet Sali, I already had arranged a place for her to hide and work.

As agreed, we met two days later, at night, outside of the fence, at the entrance to the forest. My sister arrived, bruised from the beating she had received at the hands of the camp commander. She told me that after I had fled, the commander had called her in for questioning and tried to get her to tell where I had gone. He did not spare any means to get her to tell him where I had gone.

My sister withstood the interrogation bravely. Despite the torture and beating, she showed moral and physical strength and did not reveal where I had gone. I was very grateful and admired her for that, because not everyone would have been able to withstand the torture. There were cases where it wasn't young and weak girls, such as my sister, who were involved, but adults and strong men, who broke under torture and led the murderers to places where Jews were hiding. Some members of my family were captured in that manner.

My sister tried to convince me to return to the camp but after hearing that I had found her a place to hide and that I felt that everyone in the camp was living on borrowed time because it was clear that sooner or later we would all be killed, she agreed that I was right. I took her straight to the woman who had agreed to hide her, who received her nicely and put her in the hiding place she had prepared. I returned to my farmer's house and began working. The farmer described my chores for me: I was to cut trees and chop them into small "slices" and arrange them in piles in preparation for the winter; take the cows out to pasture; help him thresh the wheat; and clean the cowshed every morning. He brought me a glass of fresh milk and a large slice of bread. I ate to my heart's content – it was like a "taste of heaven". He showed me where I would sleep. It was in a corner of the cowshed. I spread some straw out on the floor and slept there at night. I was happy.

It is clear that when I took the cows out to pasture every day, I was flirting with death, whether at the hands of one of the Ukrainians or some policeman that I might meet on the way. I did everything I was asked to do, constantly afraid and worried. But there were moments during which I would forget everything and simply enjoyed the feeling of freedom and ... a full stomach.

It was summer and I hoped that this state of affairs would last for a long time. The work was hard, particularly when I had to split large blocks of wood that were heavier than I was. I would stick the ax into the middle of the block of wood, raise it with all my strength and turn it while hitting it with the base of the ax. When the block had split into two, I would steady it on the ground with my bare foot and split it into small "slices". I became quite good at this, a real expert. When I had to help the farmer's son thresh the wheat, we would stand across from each other, each holding sticks in our hands, and we would beat the sheaves in tempo, one after the other, while the wheat spilled onto the floor. At the end of the threshing, I would gather the straw and tie it into bundles. I would sweep the wheat that remained on the floor with a large broom, shaking it to get rid of the remains of straw and pour the wheat into sacks. The days passed quickly and I was very busy, from morning to night.

Sometimes I would go visit my sister and she told me that that the woman who had taken her in was very nice to her. I would return from such a visit feeling very happy that she had a quiet corner to live and that the farmers who were putting her up were warm-hearted people. My farmer's wife once noticed that I had "disappeared" and asked me where I had been. I told her that I had been visiting my sister because I missed her and wanted to talk to her a little bit. She told me that I should be very careful because there were bad people in the village and they might inform on us. I replied that I was being very careful and that no one had seen me.

One day, the owner and his son set up a contraption in the yard to roast a whole pig for the upcoming holiday. Afterwards, they took the pig, killed it with a blow from an ax and hung it over the fire that they had lit. They stood there, turning the pig, roasting it over the fire. All of the members of the family gathered together at noon, sitting at a festive table laden with all sorts of good foods and very ceremoniously, cut slices of meat, dripping with fat, from the roasted pig. To my surprise, they also invited me to come and dine with them at the table. I was a bit embarrassed but I entered the house, sat with them, received a wooden spoon and a fork and ate with them from a large dish that was on the table. I ate some of the pig and it didn't even stick in my throat.

This was the first time in three years that I sat at a table and ate together with other people. I had forgotten what it was like. I thanked them for their generosity and returned to my daily tasks. I was responsible for all of the farm work and I carried out my duties conscientiously. The summer days were longer and so I was able to finish all my work. The members of the family treated me well. They never rebuked me or reproached me. The hardest work, as I said before, was to stand opposite the son, who was strong, while we were threshing the wheat. I had to work with the sticks, keeping up with his tempo. We had to work at an exact rhythm otherwise I could receive a strong blow to my hands.

The son told me that I was lucky that I had escaped from the camp, because they had killed many people there. It seems that I had fled from the camp just in time. But even here I didn't feel safe and always felt that danger was lurking in the background. I just didn't know where it would come from.

Autumn arrived. The days became colder and I walked around barefoot because I had no shoes.

One day, as I was taking the cows out to pasture as usual I suddenly heard the sound of approaching hooves. I turned around and saw a policeman, a member of the Ukrainian SS unit, riding a horse. He was called Schab. He was reputed to be an extremely cruel person, an abomination to the human race. Apparently, someone had informed on me. The policeman ordered me to return the cows to the farmer's house immediately. I had no choice but to go with him. When we reached the courtyard, he got off his horse and marched me to the doorway of the house. In the meantime, the woman and her son had come outside. As they watched, the policemen threw me to the ground in front of the house and began hitting me with all his strength with the butt of his rifle. I was in shock, and apparently also lost consciousness. The policeman continued to hit me on the back and the rest of my body while the woman stood next to him, begging him to stop. He paid no attention to her and raised his rifle, aiming at my head, intending give me the final blow by shooting me in the head. At the last moment, the women caught the rifle and pulled it to the side. Amazed, Schab removed his gaze from me. Taking advantage of the moment, the brave woman's strong son approached me, picked me up off of the ground, gave me a strong push and shouted: "Run!" As if awakening from a dream, I got to my feet, saw that I was near the farm gate and immediately began running, while the policeman, having recovered his senses, shot at me. I ran in a zigzag, to the right and to the left, hearing the whine of the bullets flying close to my head, but fortunately, they missed me. Mustering up the little strength I had left in me, I ran in the direction the river, crossed the river with the water up reaching up to my neck and arrived at the farmhouse where my sister was staying. She saw me wounded and hurt, and we both burst into tears. I took off my wet and torn shirt and pants and hung them up to dry, trembling with fear. My sister had to help me lay down on the straw in the barn, because the blows I had received made it difficult and painful for me to bend over.

To this day I don't know if the policeman let loose his rage on the mother and son who had done a brave deed and saved my life.

My sister and I spoke for a long time and in view of the circumstances, we decided that in order to survive, we had to find another place. We decided to return to the vicinity of Buczacz, where there were farmers in the villages who had known us when my father and mother had done business with them. My sister spoke to the farmer, the husband of the woman who had taken her in, and said that she would give him a gold watch and a ring if he would take us there. The watch had been our mother's watch. My sister had clung to this treasure in a small silver purse that my mother had once brought from Vienna, where she had been a student. Fortunately, the farmer agreed.

We set out at dawn, in a cart hitched to two horses. In order to avoid detection, the farmer stuffed me into a sack. I twisted myself into as small a "package" as possible, which was difficult for me to do since I couldn't bend my body as a result of the blows I had received. But somehow, the farmer got the sack over my head and I curled myself up in it like a fetus, but I certainly was less comfortable than one. He tied the sack as if it was a bag of horse feed and I lay there, all twisted up, relentlessly knocked around because of the twists and bends in the road. My sister sat besides the farmer, dressed like a Ukrainian girl. She was carrying forged papers stating that she was a Christian – I have no idea where she got hold of them.

This was in the beginning of December and it was terribly cold. We were traveling and suddenly I heard somebody shout: "Halt!" Two policemen approached the cart and checked the papers of the farmer and my sister. One of the policemen went to the back of the cart and with the stick in his hand, struck the sack lightly, that is, struck me. I was able to keep from crying out and he didn't suspect a thing. I thought that it was truly a miracle that I hadn't been discovered. Once again we had been saved from certain death.

We continued for a few more hours until in the evening, we finally reached the vicinity of Buczacz. We stopped in a nearby field. The farmer and my sister were barely able to get me out of the sack, because I was hurting all over my body and was very stiff. My sister gave the farmer the watch and the ring and he left us. It was dark everywhere. For the thousandth time, we found ourselves at a crossroads, not knowing which way to turn.

In the end, we arrived at the home of the same old woman who had given us refuge and taken care of us when we had been so ill. The old woman lived alone.

We asked if we could stay with her for a few days. She was very afraid but took pity on us and agreed to let us stay with her, but only for a few days. We went into the barn to rest.

I told my sister that we should split up, that it would be safer if each of us went our own separate way.

I was always the one to instigate separations. It was clear to me that my sister could not climb the ladder to the granary, which was several meters high, and hide among the piles of straw, that she would not be able to steal into a cowshed at night and sleep next to warm cows and just before dawn, once again climb up to the granary. Thanks to the false papers she had and the large cross around her neck she might be able to find work in a household, helping children out with their studies or knitting for others. This would be easier for her than for me and I did not want to be a burden to her. We rested for a few days and then, one morning, we said goodbye and parted, each going in a different direction. I was so afraid that we would never see each other again. On the other hand, it was clear that it would be easier for us to find hiding places if we were alone. No farmer would be willing to take in two people.

Looking back, I am still convinced that this was a wise decision, despite our fears that we might never see each other again. As we parted, our eyes followed each other with fear and trepidation, but we were convinced that this was the right road to take.

Many years later, when I was asked how we could leave each other so that each person went his or her own way without knowing where or in which direction, I replied that we were forced to do that several times, but somehow, despite the hardships and different experiences that each of us endured, we always managed to meet up again. Despite the danger and certain death that awaited us around every corner, in our hearts, every time we parted it was with the strong conviction that we would survive and that one day, we would once again see each other.

Both Sides of the Cow

In the days that followed, I ran and hid like a hunted animal, wounded, almost inhuman. It was a terrible winter. In order to remain alive, I would creep into farmers' barns, where I would hide during the day. At night, I would come out to find something to eat. I had no contact at all with my sister. It was only later that I found out that she had somehow managed to reach a group of eight Jewish boys from Buczacz who had formed a partisan group and were operating out of the forests at the outskirts of the city. Despite the fact that there were few of them, they were very brave and succeeded in striking hard at the enemy. They would ambush lone Germans, steal their weapons and then use them to kill. The Germans and the Ukrainian policemen were afraid of these Jewish guerillas. They would sometimes even specifically target Ukrainians who had killed Jews as well as informers who had turned Jews over to the Nazis. The members of this group, through their daring deeds, were instrumental in avenging spilled blood.

My sister joined this group as their "housekeeper", cooking, sewing and washing their clothes. In retrospect, this was fortunate for both of us. She was very organized and at a later stage, when I was very weak and cold and was on the brink of death, she saved my life by bringing me clothes and shoes.

I continued to wander, alone, always stopping in a new place. Today, I find it hard to comprehend where I found the spiritual and physical strength to do this. This just goes to show what a person can accomplish when he is left with no other choice.

In spite of all my hardships, I could understand why the farmers were afraid to hide me – if the Germans were to find this out, they would burn down their house and either deport or kill them.

While I was hiding in any kind of place that I could find, spending endless nights laying between sheaves of wheat, I often dreamed that I was being pursued and that people were shooting at me from all directions. I would be running away from them, running and falling, which they continued to shoot, and I would get on my feet again, run and once again, fall down. I tried to fight having these dreams but never succeeded in getting rid of them. They would go on for hours on end, until I would finally wake up from a deep sleep, which had been full of nightmares. When I would awaken, covered with sweat, I was tired and exhausted from the awfulness of the dreams. I continued to have similar dreams long after the liberation. Even in Israel, after my marriage, these horrible visions would often come to me. I would awake shouting, startling my wife anew each time.

The winter dominated the surroundings. Everything was locked up tightly and it became more difficult to steal into a cowshed at night in order to share the cows' warmth after having hiding under bales of hay in the granary during the day. In the evenings, I would leave the granary, being very careful. First, I would go to the window of the farmhouse, to make sure that there were no strangers present, only the members of the family. Many times, when I reached the window, I would have to stand on my tiptoes and blow on the windowpane to melt the ice so that I could see who was inside. If I saw strangers, I left immediately and went to another farmhouse. Dogs were also dangerous and I had to make sure that I selected houses that did not have dogs roaming the yard. Often a farmer's dog, or that of his neighbor would begin barking and chasing me. As I fled, I had to make sure to smooth the snow behind me in order to hide my tracks.

In many places, the farmers would open the door, and when they saw who was standing there, would slam the door in my face. At least they did not turn me in. I can count on one hand the number of farmers that helped me. In fact, the whole story of my survival turns around four or five good souls, mostly women. I really don't know why it was mostly women who were willing to help.

During my wanderings, I approached a Polish woman that I knew, by the name of Marga, and asked her for a slice of bread. She told me that my cousin Adzio was also wandering in the area. I asked that if he should contact her again, she should tell him that I would come by again a week from that same day, and hopefully we might be able to meet.

A week passed. I went to meet my cousin, somehow certain that the meeting would indeed take place. I reached the farmhouse and knocked softly on the door. Marga came out and said that my cousin Adzio was waiting for me in the cowshed. I went in. Our meeting was, as one might imagine, very emotional – we cried and hugged each other for a long time. At first, we were unable to talk. When we calmed down, he told me that after leaving us, he had reached the aunt's house in Tchortkov, but no one was there. The whole family had already been killed. He continued and told me everything that had happened to him since we had last seen each other. It was pretty similar to what I had gone through. Adzio asked me if we could stay together and help each other. "Of course", I replied – after all, there were only the two of us left in the family (with the exception of my sister). We would either survive or suffer the fate of all the others. He was a year younger than me, very weak. I may have been tougher because I had been alone from an early age and had had to handle many difficult situations. We sat talking for hours, and told each other everything that had happened to us. I told him that I had lost contact with my sister and was very worried because I did not know what had happened to her.

At dawn, we decided to climb the ladder, to the granary over the cowshed. We reached the top and saw sheaves of wheat, with seeds still in the ears. That was the way farmers did it – they would store sheaves of wheat and every time they needed some, they would take down a few bundles and thresh the wheat. We began moving the heavy bundles around in order to arrange a hiding place with the bales, so that anyone looking up would be unaware of our presence. After many efforts, we succeeded in building ourselves a small nest where we huddled together, with a bale of straw above our heads. It was the middle of winter and the cold was very bitter, less than 20 degrees below zero. We couldn't go out, and even had we been able to, we were too weak physically. I pushed my hand through the straw on the roof and collected come snow – this was the only thing we had to put into our mouths.

We stayed there for two days, until we heard footsteps entering the barn. The steps came closer to us. It turned out to be Marga's husband, who had no idea that we were hiding in his barn. He suddenly climbed the ladder, approached the pile of sheaves and stuck a pitchfork into the bundle of straw that covered us. The pitchfork pierced the straw at an angle, serving as a kind of lever, because the bales were heavy and this angle made it easier to lift the bales. If the farmer had stuck the pitchfork into the bale at any other angle, we would have been hurt. When he lifted the bale, a normal almost daily act for him, he suddenly discovered two heads under it. He was so startled that he fainted. I called Marga, who revived him. When he recovered, he shouted that we must leave the place immediately. He was truly scared to death. We begged him to let us stay at least until nightfall and promised that we would leave in the evening. After our plea and Marga's supplications, he finally agreed, if unwillingly, grumbling at his wife. At nightfall, we came down the ladder and left the barn. We were half naked and trembling from the cold. We had no idea where to go. After a short discussion, we remembered a Ukrainian farmer from Novostaftse we had known, ten kilometers away. We thought that he might be willing to take us in. We began walking, the cold wind cutting into our bodies, but we could not give ourselves the luxury of a minute's rest. After a few hours of walking, we reached the outskirts of the city. The night was clear and every figure could easily be seen from afar against the white snow.

We began walking between the houses, hunched over, trying not to be seen, when suddenly, a group of Ukrainian youths came out through one of the doors, talking and laughing. They began chasing us as soon as they saw us and finally caught us. They immediately could tell that we were Jews and began to argue how they would divide up the reward that they would receive for handing us over to the Ukrainian SS. The reward was a bag of sugar and all other luxuries. They separated us, holding us tightly by the arms and the legs, questioning us over and over again to find out where we came from and where we had been hiding. Before we even had a chance to open our mouths to say anything, they beat us mercilessly. I, of course, wouldn't reveal the truth to them and tell them about the kind woman who had helped us. So I told them that we had sneaked into some hayloft, where we lay hidden among the bales of hay until nightfall. I kept saying that the farmer, the owner, had not had any idea that we were there. The Ukrainians wanted me to show them where we had hidden. When we reached a nearby house that was isolated from others, I pointed to the barn, which was padlocked, an unusual sight in a village. They, of course, immediately understood that I had lied and once again, beat me.

In the meantime, the second group was beating my cousin Adzio until he couldn't stand it anymore and told them where we had really been. As I said before, Adzio was smaller than me and also physically weaker. I couldn't be angry with him. He led them to the courtyard of Marga's house. They told Marga to come out and she admitted that we had been in the cowshed but claimed that she had thrown us out of there. One of her sons was part of this gang and she tearfully pleaded with them to be merciful with her and to let us go. They pretended to agree but I heard them talking among themselves, saying that they would let us leave the courtyard to make her happy and then they would catch us again.

All of a sudden, they untied our hands and feet and released us. We each received a kick in the pants and began running down the hill, weak and exhausted as we were. When I saw that my cousin was going slow, I shouted to him that he should run as fast as he could. After about 500 meters, we reached the center of the village. I was in front, and my cousin slightly behind me. The Ukrainians called a pack of dogs that began barking and chasing us. Suddenly I heard my cousin shouting: "They bit me! They bit me!" I turned back, threw snow at the dogs, causing them to fall back, grabbed my cousin by the hand and we ran as if our lives depended on it, which it did, looking for a courtyard in which to hide. I saw the open door of a storeroom. I dragged Adzio inside and we hid under the piles of grain. Barely two minutes later, we heard the Ukrainians arriving and searching for us. They passed the yard at a run, looked around, didn't see us and continued running. To this day I can't understand why they didn't discover us – however, the important thing was that once again we had escaped death.

When it was finally quiet and we were sure that the hooligans were long gone, we began talking softly, trying to figure out where to go and what to do next. There was no one in this village to whom we could go and it was freezing outside, with a strong wind. We were at out wits ends. I remembered the old Polish woman who had given my sister and I shelter after we had returned to the vicinity of Buczacz. This woman lived outside of the village, alone, without any neighbors, without family. She was truly a saint. But her village was far away, how would we get there before dawn? We discussed it for a long time. After it had been quiet for two hours, we left our hiding place hesitantly. At first we lay in the snow, still afraid of being seen, and then we decided that to start walking. But we could only walk through the fields, avoiding the roads, and the snow there was soft and deep. Which way to go? Could we could find shortcuts and not get lost? We began walking south – following a gut feeling that told us that that was the right direction. The night was pitch dark and so we couldn't even find the North Star to guide us. We found ourselves sinking into the fresh snow every few steps and once, one of my shoes remained stuck in the deep snow (my shoes were several sizes too big for me). We had to pull out our shoes, which had become wet, and tie them on our feet with ropes, so that they wouldn't fall off. This was difficult to do, as our hands were almost frozen with cold.

Every once in a while, I would glance back, just to make sure that we weren't being chased. But who would be crazy enough to stick his nose out in such weather? The only thing showing in the snow was our clear, black footprints.

We had to make superhuman efforts to survive this journey. We would occasionally stop for a short rest, but we knew that if we did not continue walking, we would freeze to death in this weather, which was at least 30 degrees below zero. We walked almost the whole night, each urging the other on. After many hours of walking, I suddenly saw snow covered houses on the horizon, all looking the same. I told my cousin Adzio that that was not what I was looking for, because I was looking for a single house and not a whole village. We decided to go around the village instead of going in. We continued walking, searching for an isolated house where the old lady lived.

Dawn was breaking. I told Adzio that we should turn to the left and all of a sudden, we saw a house standing alone – this seemed to be the area we were looking for. The closer we got to the house, the more certain I was that that was where we had to go. There were many trees around the house. In the stormy winter, they looked somber and threatening. When I looked at the giant twisting branches that arose from the trees, I felt as if someone was hiding behind us. The noise of the wind blowing through the leaves did not add to my peace of mind. We were filled with fear and dread and made our way very carefully, constantly looking around. When we reached the house, dawn was just breaking.

We knocked on her door and the old lady opened it. Seeing that our noses and ears were white from frostbite she shouted "Jesus Christ. She immediately told us not to touch either our noses or our ears because it was very dangerous. She even mumbled something about the fact that they might fall off. We sat down and she put snow compresses on our faces. After a few hours, our faces began thawing out. When we felt a tingling sensation, we touched our noses and ears with trepidation and were overjoyed to find that they were still there. In the meantime, she gave us some hot chicken soup, which literally saved our lives. We stayed with her for a few days but then she too told us, sadly, that we had to leave. We understood her situation. These were terrible days, fraught with fear. The Nazi propaganda and threats sowed terror in everyone and no one could allow himself to harbor Jews.

We left her house and once again began wandering in the cold winter. We wandered from place to place, from village to village. During the day we would creep into barns and at night we would go into cowsheds and lay among the cows in an attempt to warm up. We were always hungry and the days seemed interminable. The only food we could find were occasional slices of dry bread and snow that served as water.

One day, Adzio became ill and he developed a high fever. He was weak from the flu. We found a kind and decent farmwoman – I can only remember her last name – Woyzeck (like the hero in Buchner's play) and I asked her if we could stay there for a few days, until my cousin felt better. She allowed us to stay in the cowshed. As in other cases, her husband was not aware of our presence. Every day, she brought us a large pot of potato and onion soup. I sat next to my cousin and fed him with a spoon, but he became weaker every day. I don't know whether the weakness was the result of the illness or because of the lice that sucked his blood day and night. These were large lice that came from the cows next to which we lay all the time. I felt helpless. What more could I do? I took care of my cousin, watching him become weaker every day, unable to do anything else because there was no medicine available. All I could do was feed him hot soup.

One cold night, I lay down on one side of a cow and my cousin lay weakly on the other side. We wanted to absorb the heat that the cow was giving off. Suddenly, the cow stood up. I turned over and saw that one of the cow's legs was stepping on my cousin's body. I pushed her off and whispered to him to get up, but he didn't answer me. I came closer to him and shook him but he did not respond. I spoke to him again, but he did not answer me. I feared the worst. After some hesitation, I put my ear to his heart. I could not hear a heartbeat. I listened again. Nothing. It was then that I understood that Adzio was dead. I was overcome with distress. I looked into my cousin's face. It was calm and peaceful. In a way I envied him because he had achieved eternal rest. I wanted to die, just like him, simply fall asleep and pass over into a better world. If I had stayed outside, in the snow, instead of on straw in a barn, this might very well happen to me too. I would freeze to death in my sleep, without suffering. I shook myself to rid my mind of such thoughts. "I must continue", I mumbled to myself. I wondered what I should do now. A few minutes later, I left the cowshed and knocked on the woman's house. She opened the door and I told her what had happened to my cousin. She was clasped her hands and said: "We will bury him but you must leave right away", and she closed the door.

I do not know how or where she buried my cousin Adzio.

I stood outside, in the dark, in the freezing cold, dressed only in a sweater, without a coat. The cold make its way right to the bones. I went into the cowshed, kissed my cousin goodbye on the forehead and began walking, not knowing where I was going. All I could feel was despair. I raised my hands and cried out softly: "God, release me from this suffering also." I felt desperate – all of my efforts to survive had been in vain. There was no use fighting anymore.

I walked slowly and carefully. Every step I took sounded like breaking ice and could reveal my presence, which was very dangerous. I began to think – where should I go now? This was the first time that I actually began to succumb to despair and to lose hope. Physically and emotionally exhausted, I wandered, like the eternal Jews of Christian tradition who knows not which way to turn, has no direction and who has no one to help him. Anywhere he turns, he is not wanted and repulsed, and if someone is actually willing to help out of pity and human kindness, someone identifies with the person's misery, he is terrified that members of his family might find out that a Jews is on the property and that one of them might notify the authorities and turn in the person giving refuge. There were not many farmers left to whom I could turn and ask for a piece of bread.

At night I would sneak into someone's cowshed and with the dawn, climb up into the granary where I often found shelter without the owners finding out. It was a great physical effort to climb up to the granary, move the bales of hay and arrange a hiding place and I was running out of strength. It was only by making superhuman effort that I managed to build myself a warm and cushioned nest.

I was under great tension. The least noise or someone

coming into the barn would set my whole body atremble. Maybe the farmer would climb up the ladder to take a few bales of grain for threshing, and then I would be discovered and I would suffer a bitter end. My cousin's death had affected me badly. I had felt his suffering deep down inside, and when I had been trying to help him, I could see him becoming weaker and fading away by the hour, like a candle that burns weakly, flickers and goes out.

It is difficult to put into words this feeling of total helplessness that came over me. One looked at the sky and searched for God to help him, because he knows that no salvation can come from human beings. But God did not hear, did not see, did nothing. He had disappointed me. He had let me down

I lay there, unmoving, for a whole day. Around evening, I had recovered a little bit and I went to Marga's house, the house of the woman who had always been my last hope. I knocked on her door carefully and when she opened the door and saw me, she was very happy. I went in and told her what had happened to my cousin. She shed many tears, but immediately told me that my sister had come around looking for me. I was filled with joy. She was alive – we were both still alive! I told Marga that I would try to come back in a few days and that she should tell my sister that if she could, she should bring me some warm clothing and a pair of shoes. I left quickly because I didn't want to put her in danger. I could barely walk – I was nearly at the end of my tether. I had apparently caught my cousin's illness and felt very ill and weak.

After a week of wandering in the snow and sleeping in barns, I once again returned to Marga's farm. This time, when I arrived, there were clothes and high shoes for me. My sister had come by and Marga had told her about me and what I needed. It if were not for those clothes, I don't think that I would have been able to survive this difficult winter.

Marga ordered me into the cowshed. I obeyed her. She brought me hot water and poured it into a wood barrel that she had brought from the house and placed next to a small fire that was burning to warm up the cowshed. She told me to take my clothes off and to get into the barrel with the hot water. I took off the few pieces of clothing that I was wearing, without feeling embarrassed in front of her, and entered the water. Marga brought a razor and began to shave my skull. Every time that she threw pieces of hair on the coals, I could hear the tiny explosions of the burning lice. She scrubbed my head and my whole body with soap, scraping off layers upon layers of dirt. It felt heavenly. I couldn't remember the last time I had been able to wash. When I began putting on the new clothes, I felt as if I had been reborn. It was a wonderful feeling, one I hadn't had for a long time.

I very much wanted to stay there for a while but Marga said I would have to leave at dawn because she was afraid of her husband, that very same farmer who had discovered my cousin and myself hiding in his barn and had fainted. I respected her wishes and set out with the dawn to look for another hiding place. Dressed in my new, clean clothes, wearing high shoes and rid of lice, I felt infinitely better. All of this made me feel more confident, gave me a certain amount of security, even hope. My mood had improved immensely and I found the strength to continue my battle for survival.

Today, it is difficult for me to go back and relive all of this, and I still can't understand how and where a person finds the spiritual and physical strength that gives him the hope and ability to survive in a living hell such as that. Maybe it is only the will to live that is the force that gives you strength, because the will to live and survive is more powerful and resilient than anything else, even steel. But with time, even steel sometimes wears out and becomes weakened.

I began to take an interest in what was happening at the front. Were the Russians attacking the Germans, and was there a chance that we would be liberated? Would I, one day, be a free person? I found it difficult to get any information because there was nobody for me to talk to. When I would knock on a farmer's door at nightfall, he would not allow me to enter because he was afraid. For the most part, it was the wife who would give me a slice of bread that would have to last me a day or two. I would take a small piece of bread with a snowball that served as water. This was already the second winter that I survived in this way. When I couldn't get bread, I would search the corners of the granary for wheat or grain seeds and chew this delicacy very, very slowly. It was easier during the summer because then there were trees heavy with fruit and vegetables that grew in the fields, as well as the poppies that the farmers raised in great quantities, and so I was able to enjoy a wide variety of food. In addition, in the summer I was spared the suffering of the winter cold and it was much easier for me to move from place to place.

Being able to bathe in the river also greatly improved my general feeling. I would go into the cold, but clean water. I could also wash my clothes in the river and at night, would spread them out to dry. I would wander around without clothing, as naked as the day I was born, staying hidden where no one could see me. And so I became a creature of the night. In the morning, I would get dressed in the shirt and pants that were still damp and would go find shelter in a granary.

I had become familiar with many granaries and I would move from one to the other. I would always try to choose places that didn't have dogs in the yard. Many dogs already knew me – the homeless ones, the ones that ran around loose. There were, of course the dangerous dogs, the ones that would bite, but those, for the most part, were tied up. I would stay away from these because their barking might wake up the inhabitants of the house, and then, of course, they might chase me away.

I continued to exist like that, hungry and frozen, going from cowshed to barn, from barn to cowshed, always being careful so that no one would know or even guess that I was hiding on their premises.

The severe winter of 1944 was nearing its end. One night, a farmer who I had previously known and who I felt I could trust told me that the Russians were advancing, that there was a chance that they would soon arrive in our region and free us from the grasp of the Nazi troops. I spent another month wandering and in hiding, but I was beginning to hope that there was a chance that I might survive this hell after all.

One week later, after the snow had melted and spring flowers had begun appearing here and there, I suddenly heard distant sounds – it sounded like shooting from different kinds of weapons. I understood that something was happening. I entered a farmer's home and he greeted me warmly, telling me that he had seen Germans fleeing for their lives and that the Russians were approaching. He gave me a warm meal and I could feel the smell of freedom. Outside, I could see German soldiers running up the hill, trying to get out of the city. I began to walk in the direction of Buczacz. I met very few people because when the city had become part of the front and almost everyone had been transported from there.

At the edge of the town, I saw an open door and entered one of the houses. Inside I saw a table laden with the best of everything – the Germans had apparently fled in the middle of a meal. For the first time in a very long time, I found myself sitting down at a table and I ate the good food that was there. I ate eggs, sausage, vegetables – things I had only dreamed about for years. I saw some lemons on one of the tables.

I inhaled their fragrance and put some in my pocket. I saw a mandolin in a corner. I picked it up and felt pure joy coursing through me as I played a tune on it and sang, in Yiddish, "Where shall I go?" Suddenly, a German soldier appeared in the doorway, carrying a rifle, without either a hat or coat, just standing there, bewildered. When he peered inside, I saluted him, shouting "Heil Hitler!" He became frightened and continued on his way, running away from the Russians. I was not afraid, because I knew that finding Jews was the last thing on his mind; he was more interested in saving his own life.

The next day, I went to the marketplace. Some farmers were there. I let them smell one of the lemons that I had taken. At the time lemons were very precious because they were used as a cold remedy. The farmers immediately began chasing after me, wanting to buy lemons. I exchanged the lemons for food products, which I took back to the room I had found and where I had temporarily installed myself with my new treasures.

I began to prepare myself for a new chapter in my life.

First Liberation – Second Liberation

Buczacz was almost empty. I installed myself in a room in a tall building opposite the marketplace. A few hours later, trucks arrived loaded with Russian soldiers and there was great rejoicing. People hugged and kissed the Russian soldiers. There was an atmosphere of holiday. The day we had been hoping for had finally arrived, we had been liberated from the yoke of the Nazi conquerors, we were saved, we could return to living more or less normal lives, without being afraid that the long shadow of the angel of death might be waiting for us around every corner. Some of the Russian soldiers were Jews. They were very polite and helped us as much as they could. On the other hand, some of the senior officers were also Jews, but they were afraid to make that known. A few dozen Jews who had survived the Nazi hell and had begun to return to the city stood quietly aside, while the populace warmly welcomed the liberators, but they also found themselves swept up in the general feeling of rejoicing. On the whole, most of the local population had suffered greatly under the Germans, but it goes without saying that their suffering could not compare with that of the Jews. Their difficulties during the Nazi conquest had been mostly financial; the Germans had been in the habit of requisitioning their crops and animals in order to fill the quotas that the German army had established – so many and many eggs, so may and many kilos of flour, etc. The Jews, on the other hand, had paid with their lives.

Life was still fraught with dangers. Many areas of the city had been mined by the Germans, particularly the area near the bridges. That very day, I suddenly heard the sounds of an explosion from afar. I ran with the others in the direction of the noise and it turned out that a Benno, Jewish youth, had stepped on a mine and one of his legs had been blown off. What a tragedy! For this to happen now! After having survived so much suffering, having gone through so much, only a few hours after his first taste of freedom, he had lost a leg. This taught me a lesson and I did not wander around in those areas.

I remembered that we had a distant relative living in a small house on the hill and all of a sudden, I thought I could smell the cakes she would bake. I don't know why, but I decided to go to her house. The door was open. I went in and began going through her things, not knowing what I was looking for. I didn't find anything of interest. "Maybe there's some food around" I thought to myself. Suddenly, I heard shouts outside in Ukrainian: "I'm going to kill you, Jewboy!" It was a Ukrainian who apparently lived in one of the houses in the area that had belonged to Jews and he had seen me enter the house. I ran to the window and jumped out from a height of four meters. I was barefoot and I landed onto pieces of glass that were hidden among the weeds. The glass cut the sole of my foot in two – the front half of my foot was actually hanging loose and there was much bleeding. I began to shout for help and the "goy" fled. I tore off a piece of my shirt, tied it around my foot and then, holding my foot in one hand, hopped on one leg to the city center, a distance of about one kilometer. Under any other circumstances, it would have been an amusing sight. Someone saw my foot and quickly brought someone who claimed to be a doctor. He began to sew my foot up with coarse thread, without any anesthetic. If one were to judge by the way he sewed up my wound, one would say that he had been a shoemaker. The wound eventually healed, but to this day I have conspicuous, tender scar that is seven centimeters long. The pain was terrible and my foot became very swollen but I was lucky because it was summer and I didn't need shoes.

In the meantime, my sister had also arrived to the city and we had a very emotional reunion. We sat for hours and told each other everything that had happened to us, the places we had been. It was a miracle that we had survived, that we were still alive.

My sister told me what she had been through, particularly the interrogations that she had to suffer at the hands of the Gestapo. These interrogations had been brutal and cruel, fraught with emotional and physical pressures. While torturing her, they tried to make her admit that she was a Jewess, despite the fact that she carried papers attesting to her being a pure Ukrainian. Unfortunately, she had a "Jewish" nose, which had aroused their suspicions. Needless to day, my sister did not break under this pressure. She knew the catechism by heart and could recite it for them fluently. This undoubtedly had helped her convince them that she was not a Jewess.

We decided to live in the center of the town, where all of the Jews who had survived were concentrated in a number of houses, opposite the marketplace and the splendid building that housed the city council – a relatively new building. At first we lived in one room but later took over another room so that we had a whole apartment. We slowly learned to adjust to our new life, one of freedom.

Although we were now free, my sister remained quiet and reserved, and I never saw her show any real happiness. In comparison, I, a boy of 14, was very enterprising and immediately began doing business. I was very successful and the money that I earned quickly put me in a better mood. I became friendly with a high-ranking Russian officer and became his vodka supplier. He would invite me to his home. The Russian officer lived in one of the fancy apartments that had belonged to a German general. There was a huge closet with all kinds of clothing and he proposed that I take what I want from the closet and bring him 10 bottles of vodka, good vodka. Since I was a vodka expert, I quickly agreed to the deal. I took a bag and took everything I could grab. I came home and began sorting out the clothes and discovered some very fancy women's underpants and bras, which had apparently belonged to the general's wife or mistress. I was embarrassed and set aside these pieces of intimate apparel. I brought shirts to the marketplace and they were grabbed up immediately. I received at least one bottle of vodka for each item of clothing, and sometimes I was even able to get three bottles at a time. After a while I noticed that my storeroom was filling up with bottles of vodka. I wasn't really a clothing expert, but I managed to sell everything but the underpants and the bras, since I was a bit embarrassed to show these items in public in broad daylight. Finally, I mustered my courage and took them to the market. On the way, I saw a very beautiful "shikse" standing and flirting with a young man. I approached them and offered them my merchandise but she burst out laughing and said that she didn't need underpants. The young man laughed. A few minutes later, I saw her raise her dress and they made love in a corner of the alley, in front of everyone. I suddenly understood why she didn't need the underpants – they would have been a bother, would have been in the way ….

I met a Jewish boy in the marketplace. He was older than me. I told him what I had seen and that I had come to the conclusion that "underpants are not merchandise, they won't sell." Then he explained to me that none of the village girls wore underpants but that I could sell them to the young Polish girls, who were more "refined". I remembered that when I would hide in granaries, I would often see young couples making love but I had never seen underpants. I was took the young man's advice and looked for well-dressed Polish women. Within two days, I had sold the underpants as well as the bras, but had done so for money, because the Poles in the market did not have vodka. That's how I acquired items for my business. Now I had a lot of money but nothing to buy with it, because I always received food for my wares. I gave most of the money to my sister and she hid it. Even I did not know where.

Unfortunately, this "happiness" did not last long because we began hearing rumors that two companies of German S.S. soldiers who had been surrounded by Russian troops in the Ukrainian forest had managed to break through the cordon and were advancing in our direction. Of all places, they had decided come here! Panic set in. The few Jews who had miraculously survived fled to Tarnopol, on the Russian side, with the little strength they had left. We were very weak ourselves and didn't know if we would survive this march, which led through Ukrainian villages that had yet to come to terms with the new government. The Russians told us that the Germans would only be "passing" through the region fleetingly, that they were actually retreating. While we were still hesitating, the Germans entered the city, turning the whole region into a new front. They dug trenches in the city and immediately "transferred" (expelled) the inhabitants. Thus, we once again found ourselves in a trap from which it seemed there was no escape. Not having any other choice, we joined the rest of the population that was being evacuated from the city.

We reached a small village that contained only a few isolated houses. We thought that we would be able to hide there for the time being. We approached the yard of a woman, who received us very nicely. She immediately knew that we were Jews and warned us to be careful of others in the area. "They haven't become Jew-lovers yet," she said. In the meantime, we began hearing rumors that the Gestapo was searching for the few Jews who had remained alive. My sister immediately went to hide in the field while I remained in the courtyard for a few more moments, I don't remember why. Suddenly, from afar, I saw some German soldiers drawing near and saw them catch my sister, who was fighting them, despite their superior strength. I wanted to grab a pitchfork and run to try to save her, but the Ukrainian woman stopped me at the last moment and wouldn't let me go there. She ran out to the field herself, saved my sister from the Nazis and brought her back. I still don't know how she managed to do that. This woman was in the advanced stages of pregnancy and all the women in the area gossiped about her, saying that her husband, who was in the Polish army, had been captured by the Germans and that she had become pregnant by the "holy spirit". We didn't care about the gossip and were glad to be able to hide with her. A few days later, the woman began having labor pains. She went into the barn and within an hour, came out with a crying baby in her arms.

We stayed with her for a few days, but we began feeling restless. Despite the German interdiction about residents living there, we both decided to return to Buczacz. We stayed in Buczacz along with a few other survivors. At a certain stage, my sister went out to look for food in the city, which was empty. She was caught by the Gestapo who interrogated and tortured her. Once again, my sister did not break. The cross around her neck, her false papers and her knowledge of the Christian litany saved her life again. When the Gestapo released her, she felt that she was being followed and so did not return to our bunker, but instead walked 20 kilometers away from Buczacz, finding shelter in some village (I found all this out when I saw my sister again, several weeks later, after the Russians had returned to Buczacz). A few days later, when my sister had failed to return, I became very afraid and worried that something had happened to her, and I wasn't sure if I would ever see her again, but refused to believe it. In the past also, whenever we had parted and each had gone his separate way, I always held onto the belief that we would meet again. It is difficult to explain and just as difficult to understand this kind of faith. We both faced death every day and all statistical odds pointed to the fact that we could not possibly stay alive but in spite of all that, we remained alive and always managed to find each other again.

I left Buczacz and passed through another village where I had stayed during my previous wanderings. I was familiar with all of the houses. I also knew where I could find food here. I remained hidden, hiding in a different barn every day.

One day, while I was walking through a narrow alleyway between houses, I suddenly heard shouts directed at me: "Stop! Stop!" A group of Ukrainians youths came towards me. They immediately saw that I was a Jew and began beating me. They were laughing, discussing how they were going to kill me. They played a "game" where they pushed me to the ground, tied a bullet to my head with a piece of wire, and began hitting the cartridge cap in an attempt to explode it. The bullet, which later on I found out was a dumdum bullet, exploded next to my head and wounded me. Since the explosion had wounded some of my attackers as well, they then decided to leave me alone, and continued on their way, thinking I was dead. I lay unconscious in a large puddle of blood. After about an hour, I regained consciousness. My forehead was covered with blood and my body was covered with mud.

I rose to my feet with difficulty and dragged myself over to the village well. I drew some water from the well and managed to wash my forehead somewhat, using a piece of material that I had torn from my shirt. Then, I fled to the field. Within a few days, my forehead had become swollen and my face had become infected and very swollen as well. The area around the eyes also became swollen, making it difficult for me to see. This bothered me the most because if I couldn't see, I couldn't walk. I spent most of my time lying in a barn between bales of hay. I only went out to look for something to eat when I couldn't stand the hunger anymore. I was lucky because it was the beginning of summer and it was possible to find all kinds of vegetables in the fields and in the farmers' houses – even fruits. The pain bothered me terribly, particularly the headaches which never stopped and were excruciating. The abscessed wound was full of pus. I could feel something "bubbling", seething, there on my face, striking inside of me like blows from a sledgehammer. There was no one to whom I could ask for help. The village was empty. Here and there I could see farmers who came to make sure that their homes were all right. I tried not to run into any of them because I was afraid that they would hand me over to the Gestapo. I felt that I couldn't continue anymore. I kept on trying to think of different ways to get out of this situation. I would sleep for many hours, in constant pain. I thought that this was a vicious twist of fate - the Germans hadn't managed to kill me, but a wound in my forehead was going finish me off. Every time I saw someone, they ran away because I looked like some kind of walking monster. I wandered around in this condition for about two weeks, in great pain and feeling terribly ill. A large, ugly infected lump could be seen through the swelling on my forehead. I would touch the wound every day and when I felt that the swelling had become soft, I decided to try and "operate" on myself by using a small knife that I had and cutting the wound open.

I went down to the river, where the water was clean. I took some rags from a farmer's clothesline, probably having been hung up to dry after having been used to make cheese. I approached the riverbank and cut the wound open with the small knife. Pus and blood immediately began spurting out. When I touched my forehead, I could feel something hard sticking out, as if something was imbedded in there. Every touch made me cry out in pain, but I had no choice – I grabbed the end of this "thing" and pulled it out by force. When it came out, I saw that I was holding a large fragment of the bullet cartridge. Blood continued flowing from the open wound and it was even more painful than before. I washed my forehead again with the cold water and pressed the rags to the wound, tying them in a kind of bandage around my head. I felt immediate relief.

I thought that it was a good thing that my sister had not been with me when the Ukrainian boys had caught me and exploded a dumdum bullet on my forehead. She would certainly have wanted to protect me and they would certainly have killed us both.

It was this and other "miracles" that I experienced over the years that turned me into a great believer of fate.

I kept this cartridge fragment for many years, as a talisman. It was only during the War of Independence in Israel, when the Jordanians took me captive in Gush Etzion, that I left it behind, in the Gush, because I was afraid to take it with me.

Wounded, and with my head bandaged, I continued to wander around the front lines, looking for food in the abandoned houses. Luckily, there were almost no inhabitants around because, as I said before, the farmers had been ordered to leave the battle area.

One morning, as I was walking carefully down the street, I suddenly heard the sounds of airplanes above my head. A plane appeared, flying low, spraying German army positions. The German soldiers that came out of the house opposite me signaled me to get down and take cover in the trench. It apparently never occurred to them that I might be a Jew. Instead, I ignored their warning and entered the house which they had just left. And what did I see? The Germans had been in the middle of a meal and the table was covered with food. I put everything I could lay my hands on into a bag as quickly as I could and ran towards the nearest barn, where I climbed the tall ladder. I pulled the ladder up after me to prevent them from finding me if they began searching. To this day I don't know where I found the strength to pull the heavy ladder up after me. I lay there quietly. After about 15 minutes, I heard a dog barking and shouts in German, and I immediately understood that they were indeed looking for me. They had apparently realized that I was a Jew. The dog reached the barn but lost my scent there. I didn't know it at the time – but years later I was told that if there is straw on the ground, a dog loses the scent.

At any rate, once again, at the last minute, I was saved from falling into Nazi hands. In the meantime, I had plenty of food. I was able to stay up in the hayloft for a few more days without having to come down.

Every day that passed, I thanked God that I had food and didn't have to wander around the German front, because it was very dangerous. One day I heard voices near the barn. I peered through a hole in the straw roof and saw a German officer talking to a beautiful girl. They entered the barn. I was too scared to move or even breathe. The couple began undressing. This was certainly an intriguing sight for an adolescent lad like me, but at the same time, I was frightened to death. They made love just below me, and for several hours, I had to stay as still as a rock. They finally left in the evening.

After they had left, I arose, straightened out my legs and beat my body with my hands to get the blood flowing again through my limbs. After I recovered, I decided to move on. I passed through an apple orchard and saw that there were still some apples hanging from the top of the tree. I immediately climbed to the top of the tree to pick them. I found a strong branch, sat upon it and began to eat the apples with relish, just as Adam and Eve had probably done in the Garden of Eden. After several minutes of pure heavenly bliss, I heard someone enter the orchard. I turned my head and saw a German soldier walking arm in arm with a girl, kissing and hugging her. They sat down under one of the trees. I had a feeling of déjà vu. I began to tremble in fear and I stopped breathing. If the German discovered me, he would certainly kill me on the spot. In the meantime, the couple began undressing. To tell the truth, this vision "did something" to the boy whose hormones, despite everything, were in good working order. However, as in the barn, despite the fact that I was intrigued, I was also scared to death. The couple made love for a long time, it seemed to me to be forever. When the sun had set, they finally got dressed and left. I waited for a little while, just to make sure that everything was safe and then climbed down the apple tree. Once again I had been saved. Then and there I decided that I would not climb any more trees!

I expected the Russians to attack any day because I understood that their army was stronger than the Germans. The Germans only had two divisions left in the forests of the Ukraine. Their death throes should come to an end soon. However, as is well known, a wounded beast can be very dangerous.

One day, I was awaked by the noise of cannon and machine gun fire. I understood that the Russians had begun their heavy assault upon the Germans. I opened a small chink in the straw roof and saw Russian soldiers advancing rapidly with tanks. I began to jump for joy, right there on the roof – I was free again! When the battle died down, I came down from the hayloft and went into the city.

This was on July 27, 1944. Four months of terrible and unnecessary suffering had passed since the week of that first liberation. The remaining survivors once again began to straggle back, but this time, there were even less of them, because a large number of people who had been alive when the Russians had come had been caught when the Germans had returned – caught and killed.

Two days later, my sister Sali also arrived in Buczacz!

She came together with our cousin Meltcha, whom my sister had taken care of while she was sick. They told me an interesting and fascinating tale about the way they had been saved. A German soldier had discovered them while they were hiding in a barn in a small village. He was serving in the Wehrmacht and was a goodhearted person. Despite the fact that he knew that they were Jewish, he didn't turn them over to the Gestapo and once in a while would bring them some food and medicine for the sick cousin. He even sat with them and tried to raise their spirits. Yes, such things actually happened. Even among the Germans there were those who had a conscience! Unfortunately, they were too few and far between. A small ray of light is not enough to light up the dark.

.

After the Liberation

There were very few Jews left in Buczacz and the whole atmosphere was very gloomy and sad. This time, there was no evidence of joyous expressions that had been expressed after the first liberation. I was 14 years old at that time and my sister was 21. There was no one to take care of us. But, when one is alive, a person must also make a living. I knew that Russian soldiers were "crazy" for vodka and that every farmer had a small still for making vodka. There were all kinds of vodka and I slowly became an expert regarding this alcoholic drink. I could differentiate between the different kinds of vodka according to color and smell, determine which vodka was good and could even tell what ingredients were used to make it. I traded matches and kerosene that I had gotten from somewhere for some bottles of vodka. I hired a farmer and his cart and rode to the outskirts of the city, to a water conduit under the road, where I had hidden my treasures. I only took out one bottle of vodka and went back out to the road. As soon as I neared a column of military vehicles, I raised the bottle and the whole column came to a halt. The soldiers looked at the vodka bottle in my hand as if hypnotized. Talking very politely, I asked for a jerry can of kerosene in exchange for the bottle. I must say that I was surprised that the "trick" worked and they gave me a jerry can. I saw that this system would work – I hid the jerry can under the water conduit, taking out two more tempting bottles. In this way, I was able to exchange six bottles of vodka for six jerry cans of kerosene. I called the carter and he helped me haul my treasure home. The building in which we lived had a small room in the basement which I had taken over and used as a storeroom. I padlocked the door to the storeroom, because otherwise, everything would have been stolen. I proceeded to pour the kerosene into individual bottles, making it possible for me to ask astronomical prices. I exchanged one bottle of kerosene for one bottle of vodka from the farmers – a tremendous profit.

It is difficult to imagine the Russian soldiers' passion for vodka. They would sell everything they had, even their coats, to get some. The only thing that could compete with their passion for vodka was their desire for women. The Russian soldiers were always looking for women and always managed to find some, even if they sometimes resorted to violent means to attain their goal.

I continued doing business with vodka for a while and earned a lot of money. Another very sought-after product was yeast, used to bake bread as well as to make vodka. I would buy large packages package of yeast and break them down into small packages of 50 grams each. A small package of yeast brought me a bottle of vodka!

The first days following the liberation, until the establishment of the new regime, were very unstable.

The Russians decided to make changes in the make-up of the population: Poles were sent to Poland and thousands of Ukrainians who had cooperated with the Nazis were deported to Siberia. From Russia and central Ukraine, the Russians brought loyal Ukrainian communists and settled them in place of the people they had deported. No one said a word about this "transfer" policy and whoever tried to oppose it was shot on the spot. They sent young local Ukrainians out to dismantle mines and many of them were killed while trying to do so. I did not feel any pity for them, but I remembered that among the Ukrainians there had been some, if only a very few, who had helped me during those terrible dark days.

While wandering around the city, I once saw a convoy of trucks completely filled with Ukrainian nationals being exiled to Siberia by the Russians. I turned around to look – I had always been a curious person - and suddenly, among those being deported, I saw the Ukrainian woman who had saved my life over and over again, whose son had been one of those who had caught my cousin and I on that terrible winter night. I shouted at her: "What happened? What about the rest of your family"? She then told me, crying, that her husband had been killed during the Russian bombardment and that the Russians had taken her sons to dismantle mines that had been placed in the area of the railroad tracks.

I wanted to shout to the Russian soldiers to let her go, because she had not hurt anyone, quite the contrary, but I knew that my request would go unheeded, might even put her in greater danger and my be risky for me. I could only repay her slightly for all of her good deeds. I quickly ran to the market and bought a large loaf of bread. I tried to get close to the truck to give her the bread but the soldiers guarding the truck would not let me do this and the convoy began moving. I waved goodbye to her and threw the loaf of bread into the truck, towards that good woman who was crying, who would probably never have a chance to go back to her village, and I ran down the street, crying.

After a while, my sister decided that it was time that life return to normal and she said that it was all well and good to do business, but I should also start thinking of the future. She wanted me to go to school and study.

The Russians opened a school in a big house on one of the estates and I began to study there. I found that I was the only Jew among the students who were either Ukrainian or Polish. In view of my previous experience, I was not exactly enthusiastic about this situation. I had mixed feelings about school. On the one hand, I thought that I had lost four years of schooling that are normally the basis for continuing on to higher studies, and now I had an opportunity to make up for lost time. I was also very curious and had a great thirst for knowledge. I particularly liked the singing and dancing lessons, especially the kazatchok.

However, while sitting in class and listening to the teacher, I suddenly found myself thinking about the family which was no longer and all of the experiences in my life. The teacher looked at me and he noticed that I wasn't paying attention. He called me to the teachers' room and asked me if there was something bothering me. "Why are you so serious and why do you always look so sad?" he asked. I told him that I was not like the other boys, that the Germans had, among other things, robbed me of the best period of my life, my youth, and that it was difficult for me to concentrate and listen, because I had lived like a hunted animal for so many years, and the transition from one kind of life to another had been too hasty. Apparently more time would have to pass until I could get used to my new situation.

I told him some of what I had gone through. He nodded his head in sympathy and told me to come to him whenever something or someone bothered me, or if I had any difficulties. The teacher added: "It's good to see that you enjoy the singing and dancing classes. You have a pleasant voice and you're not bad looking. It looks as if some of the girls, particularly the pretty ones, keep making eyes at you all the time."

I blushed a bit. He was right, I had also noticed the looks of affection thrown at me by the girls. They even used to follow me after school. I used to wander around the depressing city, its houses empty of inhabitants, most of whom had been murdered. When I would wander around the gloomy buildings, most of which had been destroyed, I would often sense that those girls were preparing to "ambush" me. They would peer around the gray walls but as soon as I would turn in their direction, they would giggle and hide.

At that time, girls weren't first and foremost on my mind, because my life was at a crossroads. I was unsure as to my future. In the evenings, some young people my sister's age would gather at our house. I would listen to their conversations. Most of them said that they had decided to leave Buczacz and go to Eretz Yisrael, where the refugees that had remained alive would gather and where we would build our new home, among Jews, build a state of our own where we could finally be free, after two thousand years of exile. Why stay here, in this huge graveyard? Everywhere we went in Buczacz we could see ground soaked with the blood of men, women and children, whose cries could still be heard, hanging in the air. Just because the Germans had lost the war did not mean that anti-Semitism had disappeared - it had not stopped for a single day. We could not travel to the villages where our families had lived and try to find out if anyone had survived. It was too dangerous. We knew that such hope was faint, because had someone survived, they would probably have come to Buczacz.

My sister and I discussed this at length and felt, as did the others, that it would soon be necessary to leave the city, because we there was no future for us in Buczacz.

A few months later, my sister and I decided that this empty, ruined city held nothing for us and we began to make preparations to leave. This didn't take long because we had very little to pack. We decided to advance with the Russian army in the direction of Romania. I hoped that I would be able to fulfill my longtime dream of reaching the Land of Israel, thus fulfilling my teacher's last wishes.

We rose at dawn and went to the train station. We had divided our money between the two of us so that if one of us were to be robbed, the damage would not be so serious. There was a great crowd at the train station. Russian soldiers traveling to the front, to Germany, filled the railroad cars, because there, the war was still going on. We gave the conductor some money and he got us onto the train. We traveled in the direction of Peshmishel, a city on the Polish-Ukrainian border. We got off the train in Peshmishel and looked for the local Jewish community. They gave us a place to stay for a few days, while we planned the next stage of our journey.

We took advantage of the great confusion that reigned and crossed the border illegally into Hungary on a train filled only with Russian soldiers. I played the role of my sister's bodyguard to prevent them from bothering her. I did my duty faithfully, keeping close to my sister at all times, and I have to say that luckily, we did not run into any problems.

We reached a city called Satmar (the spiritual center of a large Hassidic community). There too, we looked for the Jewish community. We reached the community's center and arranged to stay there a few days. It was difficult for me to speak to them because they spoke Hungarian but I always managed to find someone who spoke Russian.

At noon, we went to the community's restaurant to eat lunch and were witness to a heartbreaking scene. A girl who had just been released from a concentration camp came in and was told that her whole family had been exterminated. In front of everyone, she began to scream and behave wildly. She seemed to have suddenly gone out of her mind. It was a very hard thing to see. Some of the men in the restaurant overpowered her and took her to the hospital.

We wandered around the city for a few more days and decided to go to Bucharest, the capital of Romania. We were very fortunate because we had a nice sum of money, the profits from my vodka enterprise. We went to the Satmar train station and it was the same story all over again – no room for civilians on the trains. I slipped some money into the conductor's hand and we finally found ourselves on our way to Bucharest.

When we reached Bucharest, we were sent to the Joint [a Jewish help organization] and were told there that there was a group of Jewish children who were studying agriculture with the purpose of immigrating to Israel. I was very enthusiastic about joining them because I really didn't want to stay in the company of adults all the time (my sister was much older than me. She was already a woman while I, despite everything I had gone through, everything I had done, was still only a boy of fourteen and a half). I also felt that I was a burden to my sister and holding her back. Anyway, I felt that staying in that institution would a step forward to help me fulfill my dream, that of "going up" to the

Land of Israel.

I went there with my sister, to the outskirts of the city. There it was – green and beautiful fields and the youth group, headed by Dr. Brettler and his wife.

When we reached the institution, Dr. Brettler interviewed me. He was very polite and it turned out that he had come from our area, from a city not too far from Buczacz. There was an immediate bond between us. The institution, called "Banyasa" looked very organized and I was enchanted by it. I told my sister that I wanted to stay there. I gave her all the money I had left in my pockets and she went back to the city.

My sister came to visit me a few days later. She told me that she was considering joining a group of friends who had decided to go to Italy. "This time" I told her, "we're really reaching a parting of the ways, because I will soon be going to the Land of Israel and you must join your friends, the group of people your age, from Buczacz, and go with them to Italy. You have your life to lead and I must lead mine."

My sister wept and once again, we went our separate ways – this time, for a long time. We were not to see each other for fifteen years. Once again I was alone, but this time, I felt secure and full of hope.

My sister Sali did reach Italy. She stayed several months in Bari, in a transit camp for refugees who had survived the war. There she married a Jew, a Pole from Krakow. Sali contacted our relatives in the United States and our uncle sent her immigration papers. In 1948, my sister Sali and her husband reached the shores of the "land of unlimited opportunities."

I quickly adjusted to life in the institution: half a day would be spent studying, and the other half would be spent working on a large nearby farm which belong to the Banyasa Agricultural School. The group of children to which I was assigned was already very close knit, because they had been together for some time – a group of Polish children who had survived the war and come together in Budapest. We wore a green uniform that consisted of short pants, a shirt, a kerchief and a scout cap. We would march down the street in perfect order, singing Russian marching songs. I was the one who introduced this custom. I would sing a solo and then they would all join me in the chorus. We were very proud when passers-by looked at us in wonder.

Myself (in circle) in Dr. Brettler's youth group, Bucharest, May 1945

This was the beginning of a new chapter in my life, one filled with optimism. For the first time in longer than I could remember, I again felt that I might be able fulfill my dream, the one my old teacher in the Buczacz ghetto and I used to talk about. I remembered my promise – I would survive and reach the Land of Israel, the land promised to us by God.

These were happy months for me but at the same time, my heart was full of sadness. I could not escape my memories. I could not forget the days filled with atrocities that I had experienced, images of which appeared, like recurring nightmares, day and night, and even if I was happy, time was too short to heal the emotional and physical wounds that I had received during the war.

Very warm and close friendships developed among the youths led by the Brettlers. We enjoyed a feeling of fellowship and warmth. We sang songs about the Land of Israel, danced folk dances and romantic relationships also developed. After all, we were only 15, 16 years old. Dr. Brettler and his wife ran an exemplary institution. They were both very devoted to the group and exhibited great patience and devotion. They saw their work as a dedicated mission and prepared us for our voyage to the Land of Israel in the same way. Both our agriculture studies and our regular studies were an excellent preparation for our imminent voyage to the Land of Israel.

During the months I spent in that institution, I eagerly drank in every word about the Land of Israel and about what awaited us there. At the time, the British governed the country which they called Palestine and they would not let even the survivors of the Holocaust in Europe, enter. They only issued a few immigration permits (certificates) for youths. Very few young survivors were lucky enough to receive such a "certificate".

There was much anticipation in the institution because we had been told that we would be receiving some of these immigration certificates and we felt that the dream of immigrating to the Land of Israel was finally becoming a reality.

Our institution received only a few "certificates" at the end of the year, but the veteran and well-knit "Hungarians" group had priority. A lottery was held for the remainder of the certificates among the rest of the youths who had gravitated to the institution from all areas of Europe. My name did not come up.

The immigrant ship was anchored in the port of Constanza, in Romania, and the group prepared to travel to the port by train. Those of us who had been unlucky in the draw and had not received certificates, did not give up and decided to accompany them by train to Constanza. When we reached the port, the "lucky" ones boarded the ship while the rest of us, those who were staying behind, stood by sadly, looking at the ship, dreaming that one day, they too would be boarding a ship for the Land of Israel.

When it began to grow dark, we realized that the ship was tied up alongside the dock. We noticed the round windows of the cabins along the ship's stern and thought that it might be possible to open them. We crept close to the ship under the cover of darkness and asked our friends, who were already on board, to open a window from the inside. When they had done that, we approached the windows and, one after the other, began to jump into the ship. I jumped, but before I even managed to get back on my feet, someone grabbed me by the collar – it was a Romanian sailor. I jumped up and turning around very fast, freed myself from his grasp. I ran around onto the ship's deck until I found a place to hide under a pile of the group's bundles.

A few hours later, I heard the whistle announcing the ship's departure and it began moving away from the dock as it sailed out to sea. I felt that it was safe for me to come out of hiding and join the group. There was nothing more to fear from anyone, because we were now on the open sea.

During the voyage, we would sit with Dr. Brettler and enthusiastically drink in stories about the Land of Israel, the settlements, the kibbutzim and the first Halutzim [pioneers] who fought off malaria, defended themselves against the riots provoked by the Arabs, and who proved themselves to be determined and resolute in their attempts to hold on to their land at all costs. We were fascinated by these stories and couldn't wait to reach the shores of the Land of Israel.

The sea trip greatly improved my emotional and physical condition. The fresh sea air increased my appetite. Unfortunately, some of my comrades suffered from seasickness. They threw up and were unable to eat. As a result, there was a lot of food for those who felt fine, like me, and I took full advantage of the situation.

Thus began my journey to the Land of Israel, the land of my dreams.

In the Land of Israel
and "Mikveh Yisrael"

After a few days of calm and quiet sailing, we reached the port of Haifa in the evening. It was an amazing sight! The mountain glittered with the lights of houses. The ships next to us rocked silently, just like in fairy tales. Everything was beautiful. We thought that we had finally reached the safe haven we had been dreaming about for so many years.

We rose at dawn and got dressed. We were told that the British had already been informed that there were some "illegal" children on the ship. It seems that the Romanian captain had informed them. The British were getting ready to board the ship and remove us by force. We were told that members of the Haganah would be coming on board to help us get off the ship rather than have us fall into the hands of the British. We were told to dress in khaki shorts and kova tembels (an ordinary hat which symbolized Israelis at the time) so that we could pretend to be port workers.

After changing clothes, we came up on deck and helped remove the cargo from the ship. A member of the Haganah who stood next to the cable that was hanging down told us to sit on the cargo so that the crane could lower us, without anyone noticing.

After the first youth had left the ship in that manner, the British "caught on" and the rescue operation came to a halt. As we were standing around, wondering what to do, we suddenly saw many British soldiers on the deck. We ran from them. We were all ordered to enter one cabin. We locked ourselves in and refused to come out. We sat, crowded in that cabin, shoulders touching, and began singing Israeli songs. We sang "Hevenu Shalom Aleichem" over and over again.

Someone from the Haganah came in the evening and told us that the British had decided to take us to the Atlit camp, and that we were to follow their orders. There was to be no question of resistance.

We left the ship in an orderly manner and they put us in a truck that took us directly to the camp in Atlit, near Haifa. It was hard, but one thing gave us comfort – our lives were not in danger.

Within a very short time, we had organized ourselves in the camp. We improved our knowledge of the language. Back in Romania, we had studied Hebrew during the few months we had spent in the institution, so that each of us could, more or less, understand what was being said to him / her. We played various sports – soccer, basketball, etc. We were very closely guarded because a Palmach unit had carried out a rescue operation a few months before our arrival,. They had broken into the camp and released new immigrants interned in the camp.

We were promised that we would be released very soon. And indeed, after a few weeks, we were told that we free to go. I have no idea how this was arranged, but it didn't matter – we were happy to be getting out of the camp.

After our release, the British stopped interning illegal immigrants in the Atlit camp but instead, sent all of those arriving illegally to the shores of the Land of Israel to camps in Cyprus. This was a cruel and brutal thing to do especially since this action was accompanied by brutal behavior on the part of the British soldiers. They put Holocaust survivors behind barbed wire fences, forcing them to relive the horrors they had recently undergone in the concentration camps. Any feelings of freedom and liberation they might have had with the Liberation at the end of World War II disappeared as if they had never existed. These British were, in fact, the very same "gentlemen" who today preach morality to us when we attempt to protect ourselves from cruel murderers whose goal is to annihilate us.

The Jewish Agency sent a truck to the Atlit camp and when it arrived, we all piled in and began traveling. We had no idea where we were headed. On the way, we saw glimpses of the Israeli landscape and that warmed the hidden corners of our hearts. In the middle of our journey, we stopped in Kibbutz Ma'agan Michael. We were told that the British were coming to search for secret weapons stores hidden in the kibbutz and it was up to us to disrupt the search as much as possible. Upon receiving our orders we got off the truck and began running all around, all over the kibbutz. Thus we found ourselves involved in our first Palmach operation.

We climbed back in the truck in the evening, tired out from running around, and we continued our travel in the direction of the agricultural school in Magdiel. When we reached the schoolyard, we were greeted with songs and dances. We were excited to find some of our friends from Romania. We all went to the dining room and were given a banquet fit for a king.

In Magdiel we were informed that in the meantime, the rest of the group that had come with us "legally" on the ship had been transferred to "Mikveh Yisrael". We, of course, asked that we also be allowed to join them.

Within a few weeks, we were taken to join our group in "Mikveh Yisrael". Our friends told us about their adjustment to the school. We were a very close-knit group, probably because of all the suffering we had all undergone. Each of us carried within our hearts and our minds the complex memories of the struggle for survival. But in moments of joy, we would allow ourselves to open ourselves to enjoying it.

It might seem peculiar, but I cannot remember ever witnessing an argument within our group. We were unusually patient with each other and showed great sensitivity and understanding. Everyone made an effort not to wound or insult the others. We accepted each other as we were – with all our good and bad points. We truly followed the precept of "love thy brother as thyself". If we suddenly saw that one of our comrades was in a bad mood, we would ask what happened and try to help and provide encouragement. Everyone had moments during which he or she would think of their home and their parents. "Why them and not us" was a question that often preoccupied us. This dilemma could be seen in facial expressions and sudden silence.

In "Mikveh Yisrael", I felt that I had been reborn. I knew that I had missed the joy of adolescence, the years during which the soul of a youth is shaped. Living as I had, like an hunted animal, facing inhumanity everywhere I turned, without hope and without a future, without a home, parents, love or human warmth and kindness – all of the things which every normal child takes for granted. I had also missed out on all those years during which schooling provides a basic education and instead, had spent those years in the ghetto or wandering from village to village.

Here, in "Mikveh Yisrael", I began a new chapter in my life – this was an emotional, physical and spiritual rebirth. Here, I was taught the wonderful values of love for one's country, for the Torah and for work, and as I said earlier, the invaluable precept of "love thy brother as thyself". In "Mikveh Yisrael", I was given a new lease on life and adopted as mine the dream of establishing a country for the Jewish people, the vision of the ingathering and the coming together of the exiles. These were the educational values which I had been taught as a child, before the war.

The "Mikveh Yisrael" agricultural school had a wonderful teaching staff that provided all subjects. The teachers took the trouble to expose us to as many areas of study as possible, as well as instilling in us the values of Judaism and altruism.

The children in "Mikveh Yisrael" were divided into two sectors: the "religious" and the "liberal" sectors. Children who were considered to be religious would study all of the subjects, but particular emphasis was placed on Jewish studies. The separation into sectors was rather arbitrary, and the students were not necessarily classified as "religious" because of their beliefs, or because they had come from observant homes. Our class belonged to the "religious sector" and every Shabbat, we would study the Torah portion for the week and all relevant interpretations. I very much enjoyed these sessions because I was anxious to regain those values which I had once been taught and which I had forgotten over the years. These studied often brought to mind the beloved teacher of my younger years.

Sometimes, Professor Yishayahu Leibowitz would come on Shabbat. He would discuss the issue of "Church and State" with us. I particularly recall these lectures, because this was in the beginning of 1946, before the establishment of the State, and it was a very important and much debated issue between secular and religious persons who were wondering what would be the Jewish character in the new State. The question was: would Halacha (Jewish Law) determine the lifestyle of each and every person, and to what extent? I feel that Prof. Leibowitz was right when he supported a separation of "Church and State". It is truly unfortunate that our leaders did not accept his point of view – had they done so, things might look different today, in view of what is happening to us when religion, as promoted by the religious politicians, have an undue influence upon the character of the 3tate of Israel. The religious hatred and gap that is part of Israeli society today are the direct result of this.

It is true that I stopped believing in God during the Holocaust. I was angry with Him because I couldn't understand how He could look down from on high, see what has happening to the Jews, and sit by idly, doing nothing. However, when I was told that I was to join the religious sector in "Mikveh", I did not protest or disobey my instructors. I saw this as a kind of return to my father's hearth and was happy that I had been given an opportunity to complete part of my Judaism studies that I had had to forego because of the war.

Today, I truly believe that there is some kind of supreme force and that God is to be found in the heart of every person, particularly when they do good deeds towards their fellowman and if they are always willing to help one another. I do not believe in the God of organized religion, but I do not consider myself a skeptic.

During the week, we would work half a day and spend half a day studying. Our group continued to be guided by the late Dr. Brettler, who had been with us back in Banyasa and in Bucharest and who had prepared us for coming to Israel.

We felt wonderful – here, we were free, living without fear, no longer living under the executioners' shadow which had haunted us everywhere we went. I thirsted to learn everything and I very much enjoyed this feeling of freedom after having been constantly hunted and persecuted simply because I had been born a Jew.

Only one thing diminished my great joy at being in "Mikveh Yisrael". A short time after my arrival and before I had become adjusted to the place, I began suffering from very strong headaches, apparently a type of migraine, particularly in the mornings. I was often forced to leave the classroom in the middle of lessons because I could not stand the pain. I would go to the botanical garden and to sit there on a bench for hours, looking at the beautiful plants around me, until the pain would pass and I could finally feel some relief. The pains were concentrated in the area of the forehead. I went to the infirmary but none of the medications brought me relief. I was even sent for head X-rays, but they couldn't find anything. I attributed these pains to the bullet wound dating back to when the Ukrainians had exploded a dumdum bullet next to my head. I still bear a very prominent scar on my forehead and it is still sensitive to the touch. I have often been asked about this bump on my forehead, whether it was a war wound. I always said that I had received a blow on my forehead. I have never been able to bring myself to tell any the real story, not even my family.

On the whole, I almost never spoke of what had happened to me, not even during my stay in "Mikveh" or in the years to come. I was determined not to talk about the horrible things that I had had to endure. I just couldn't share these with anyone – I determinedly ignored any attempts to draw me out about that period. I did not want anyone pitying me, not even for a moment. I constantly told myself that I would concentrate on the future, not on the past. I buried the past deep inside of me.

While sitting in the botanical gardens of "Mikveh", I could see myself, back there, lying on the ground with my head in a pool of blood and the Ukrainians laughing. However, when I looked around and saw the trees, the plants and the butterflies, I would "wake up" to the reality of the present. I comforted myself with the thought that I was now free and living in a country of my own.

I eagerly waited all week for Friday evening to come around. After dinner, we would get together and dance folk dances. In honor of Friday night, Shabbat, I would prepare my beautiful Russian shirt, polish my shoes and feel that I looked very festive. I owned one pair of high-top work shoes and a pair for Shabbat, low-cut shoes. This was sufficient for me and I was content. We would sing and dance until the wee hours of the night. I liked dancing with some of the girls but didn't develop any real romantic relationships. The "religious" sector had high moral standards and teachers and instructors kept a strict eye on us. Girls who did not follow the rules got into trouble and were expelled from the school. So the boys, too, were careful. If I got myself involved in a fling and were expelled from school, where would I go? This would ruin any chance of achieving the future that I had chosen for myself.

I decided to study the subject of irrigated crops because I was fascinated by the process of plowing and harvest. On Shavuot, it was a tradition to hold a harvesting competition in which I always participated. I even managed to set some records.

The second topic of study that interested me was blacksmithing, taught by Reuven. We would make horseshoes, various pieces of equipment and parts for agricultural machines. Reuven was very meticulous. When he held a piece of white-hot metal in the tongs, I was supposed to strike the metal quickly at a steady pace as long as it was white-hot, so that the metal could quickly acquire the desired form of the final product. The rhythm of the hammer had to be exact, depending on the rhythm that Reuven set by turning the object on the anvil, turning the tongs holding the final product on the anvil every once in a while. If, God forbid, I didn't keep up with him, I would receive a blow on the back of the neck. It goes without saying that I accepted these blows in good humor. I felt that we were creating pieces of art by taking a simple piece of metal and turning it into a useful item, sometimes even an attractive one. The smithy had a coal fireplace and bellows. I shall never forget how we would put a piece of metal into the fire until it became very red, and then take it out with the tongs, whereupon Reuven turned the metal continuously while I hit it, until, within only a few minutes, it quickly turned into a horseshoe. An added benefit from this work, in addition to learning a trade, was that the muscles in my hands became very developed and large. I was very proud of that. Every once in a while I would display these symbols of manliness to the girls.

The blacksmith's neighbor was David Leibowitz, who taught precision mechanics. He had lathes and machines for shaping metal and the like. During the War of Independence, David created the "Davidka", a makeshift mortar which was used in Jerusalem and in other places in the country. (Today, one of these stands in the center of Jerusalem, in the Davidka Square.) Later, when we had been captured and were being held in Jordan after the fall of Gush Etzion, Jordanian soldiers told us that they knew that the Jews had an "atomic bomb". This was the assumption made by the Arabs after having been shelled by the Davidka, which was very noisy and spread fear and terror among the Arabs.

Most of the teachers at "Mikveh" had come from Russia and a few had come from Germany. The Russian immigration had brought with it many intelligent people who not only contributed much of their knowledge and talents to this school, but also, for example, to the "Habima" theater – one such example was the actress Hannah Robinah, who had already been a legend in Russia.

Several times a year, they took us to theatres in Tel Aviv, among them to "Habimah". There we saw Sholom Anski's play, "The Dybbuk", starring Hannah

Robinah and Aharon Meskin, which left a great impression on me. For us, watching plays was a very exciting and infrequent occasion – we had no other way of being able to go see plays on our own, mainly because of lack of money and transportation.

I also worked in the orchards during the fruit-picking season, eating large amounts of oranges. The smell and taste of the oranges simply overwhelmed me. As a matter of fact, I loved all the work and the atmosphere in "Mikveh". I also worked in the cattle shed. Occasionally, I would go out to gather fodder for the cows. I enjoyed the smell of the freshly cut clover and this pleasing scent always put me in a good mood.

In addition to work and studies, we were also recruited into the "Haganah", the military arm of the Yishuv. We spent many hours training in hand-to-hand combat. We were given a long stick made from a branch of the bitter orange tree, with a round ball carved out at the end. We would roam the orchards for hours, looking for suitably straight branches. I have to admit that these training sessions were not pleasant. We would stand in front of the instructor and he would flay out in all directions, and if we weren't quick enough to defend ourselves with our sticks, we received a painful blow. The fact that we understood the reasons behind the blows did not make the pain any easier to bear.

We waited impatiently for the day that we would be sworn into the Haganah. It took place at night, in a clearing in the middle of the orchards that was lit by torches. We felt like the Knights of the Round Table in King Arthur's Court. We stood there with our sticks and swore, our hands on a Bible, to defend the land and the people. The feeling of awe, of wonder that was generated that night stayed with us for a long time.

Night swearing-in ceremony for the Haganah, Mikveh Yisrael, 1946.

There were very intensive underground activities related to the Haganah in "Mikveh", whether they involved training exercises or hiding weapons in "slicks", special hiding places prepared especially for this purpose. Some of the buildings in the school were very old, with deep and secret cellars, and of course, many orange groves all around. The place covered thousands of dunams (four dunams = one acre) and was located relatively near to Tel Aviv. Therefore, it was very convenient for the Haganah to use the place for a variety of purposes. The British, who "smelled" that something was going on, would often come to the school to search for weapons. We would then be told to leave the classrooms in order to create confusion during the searches.

On "Black Shabbat", when the British imprisoned almost the entire Zionist leadership, some of our leaders escaped and came to "Mikveh" to hide. Among them were Rabbi Shapira, Burg, Shprinzak and others. As I said earlier, there was no lack of hiding places in "Mikveh".

Most of the students in the "liberal" sector were children who had been born in Palestine – they came from kibbutzim and moshavim, as well as from urban areas. They displayed a certain amount of arrogance in regards to us, the ones who had come from the Diaspora. But all in all, they were a marvelous group. They behaved differently than us – we were more reserved, quiet, while they were freer, in all senses of the word. I became friends with many of them, because they knew how to enjoy life and exhibited a kind of frankness that I admired. I have remained friends with two of them. One of them was the late Amnon Carmeli, who used to tell us stories about Petach Tikva, the two of us doubling up with laughter. He was a cheerful person, with a healthy sense of humor. Even many years later, during his last moments, he continued to relate his fascinating stories when I went to visit him at the hospital, instead of me cheering him up.

The second person was Yigal Shoham, a wonderful person, pleasant and a real "Sabra" (native born Israeli).

The members of the "liberal" sector went on to join settlements and the Palmach. Many of them fell during the War of Independence. Do such people still exist today?

During the summer of 1946, we had our first annual vacation – two whole weeks – to which I had been looking forward with impatience. I was planning to work during those two weeks and earn some money so that I could buy myself a watch – my life's dream. When my vacation began, I went to Tel Aviv on foot and wandered around the streets until I found a building that was being constructed, next to the Municipal Zoo, on the corner of Shlomo Hamelekh Street. I went looking for the contractor. When I found him, I asked him if I could work for him. Fortunately, he agreed to take me on. Being naïve and inexperienced, I didn't even ask him how much I would be earning – I trusted people. This naivety is still part of my nature (and at times I have paid a heavy and painful price for it – but what can I do – it's part and parcel of me).

I did all kinds of jobs – mixing cement, carrying blocks on my back to the third and fourth floors. I did not complain, because there was no one to complain to. I kept working diligently. I had a goal! At the end of the day, I waited apprehensively for them to tell me whether I could come and work the next day. When I was finally told that I could continue, I was delighted. The next day, I woke up early in order to get to work on time.

When I arrived, I was told that the roof would be poured that day and that everybody was to work on that. We worked at a murderous pace. I carried gravel and sand to the cement mixer. We finished pouring the roof early in the evening. It was customary for the owner, the contractor, to provide food and drink to celebrate the completion of the pouring of the roof. I took part in the celebration. I didn't drink beer but the "gazoz" (carbonated water with fruit syrup) tasted very good. There was a friendly atmosphere, everyone was pleased – we had put up a roof in Israel. I know that this last phrase sounds like a cliché, but that's truly how we felt. We really felt that we were building home is the Land of Israel.

I worked there for two weeks – I would return to "Mikveh" every evening (on foot, after a hard day's work), white and dusty from the building materials and it goes without saying that I would head straight for the showers and luxuriate under the water.

At the end of the first week, on Friday, I received my wages and ran directly to the watchmaker's shop window to see if I had enough money for the watch. I made a rapid calculation and saw that I would not have enough money to purchase the leather guard to protect the watch (as was the custom at the time) as well, and without the leather guard, the watch would not be complete. The next morning, I asked the supervisor if I could work overtime during the next week so that I would earn enough money for the watch guard. He agreed, making me very happy.

A week later, after receiving my wages, I ran to the shop and bought the watch that I had coveted. I put it on with trembling hands. I was in seventh heaven. Now I felt just like all the other youths who were so proud of their watches. They had relatives and families in Israel. They would go visit their relatives and be spoiled. I had had to look for work because I had never received an allowance from anyone. I wanted to be like everyone else – we would sometimes go roaming in Tel Aviv, on Allenby Street, and would reach Whitman (ice cream shop). I wanted to be able to have at least a few pennies to be able to buy gazoz, like the others. I always found some kind of work. Even back then I knew that if one is not particular and is willing to accept any work offered, he would always be able to work. When I worked in Tel Aviv, I would always return to "Mikveh" to sleep. I never stayed in Tel Aviv overnight, simply because there was no one with whom I could stay.

Some of the vacations were spent training with the "Haganah". The "Haganah" would send instructors and we practiced wrestling, hand-to-hand combat, and conducted day field exercises and night field exercises.

I remember that day, I entered a tent during lunch break to rest and fell asleep. I woke up, feeling that someone had been watching me sleep. When I opened my eyes, I met the eyes of our instructor, who was older than me. She was very pretty, a breath of spring, and her name was Zeeva. The other instructor was called Sarah. Zeeva looked at me affectionately and said that she had been standing there for quite some time, looking at me. She added that I had especially long and beautiful eyelashes. I felt new feelings stirring in me, but I was several years younger than her and still very bashful.

During one of our vacations, we went to train in the Zefat Mountains, in a settlement called Birya. We prepared all of our equipment in the evening so as to be ready for our trip to the Galilee in the morning. The truck arrived at dawn, and we boarded it immediately, arranging our backpacks so that we could sit on them. It was very crowded. The driver was short and fat, wearing a "kova tembel" on his head and the vehicle was a "deluxe junk heap". It took us hours to reach the ascent to Zefat. The driver stopped the truck and told us to get off and start pushing, because it couldn't make it on its own. We took up the challenge, rotating places every so often, and with a combined effort, reached the top and continued on to Birya. When we got there, we showered, ate dinner and lay down to sleep in our sleeping bags.

The next morning, we began a series of day and night exercises as well as close combat training. After the tiring training sessions, we went home. Going home, we had another surprise waiting for us: at the beginning of the descent, the driver told us to get off the truck. He told us that the truck's brakes were not very good and we would have to help him slow the truck down. We had hobnailed shoes, which made it possible for us to slide down the road, slowly braking the truck, until we finally reached the bottom,

completely exhausted. We then continued on our way
back to "Mikveh Yisrael".

Two and a half years later, having finished our
studies, we held endless discussions regarding our
future, until we decided to organize into a religious
settlement group and decided to join Kibbutz Massuot
Yitzhak in Gush Etzion, in the Jerusalem Mountains.
We saw this as a great challenge from all aspects.

We had a farewell party for which we prepared a
play – a very impressive end to our studies. I also took
part, singing a solo – "The Town is Burning". The
audience was astounded by my voice and I received
many compliments all around. The play was put on at
night, in the eucalyptus grove, the "stage" lit by
kerosene lamps. It was a very festive evening and thus,
I said farewell to the most wonderful period of my life.

The next day we got on the bus and traveled to
"Massuot Yitzhat", stopping in Jerusalem on the way.
We had a few free hours and used them to walk around
the city. We walked through the Old City, with its
narrow alleyways and shops on the way the Wailing
Wall. The Arab shopkeepers offered souvenirs and
every alley was lined with countless old homes of
different styles, painted all the colors of the rainbow.
With every step I took, I thought – I am walking along
the very same historical holy places that are holy to the
people of Israel. Despite the temptations surrounding
us, we did not linger, because we wanted to reach the
Wailing Wall as fast as possible.

We could feel that access to the Wailing Wall could

be dangerous. Some of the Arab merchants threw us unfriendly looks when we passed them. I had already heard stories of how Arabs fell upon Jews making their way to the holiest place for Jews.

When we reached the Wailing Wall, the high wall with its huge rocks and utter quiet, moved us to tears. Each of us silently placed a folded up note containing our most secret wishes in cracks in the Wall.

Afterwards, we once again passed through the alleyways, walking more slowly and taking the time to look in the shops. We took in the smell of the spices and wondered at the jewelry, the copper utensils, the carpets, the embroidered clothing and handmade objects. Our mouths watered when we saw the sheep carcasses hanging on metal hooks.

And so we walked around with all of our possessions on our backs. I thought to myself – I am actually in the city about which the Jews have dreamed and prayed for 2,000 years! The city that my teacher had spoken about so much. Our dream had come true!

At the end of our tour of Jerusalem, we slowly straggled back to where the bus was waiting for us. We got on and continued our journey to kibbutz "Massuot Yitzhak".

"Massuot Yitzhak"

We were very excited to be on the bus taking us to "Massuot Yitzhak" in Gush Etzion. This was the fulfillment of my dream – to work the land in Israel, to conquer the wilderness, to settle the land and dig my roots deep into the mountain.

We were not the first to go to the "Gush" to settle the land there. In the not too distant past, private persons had purchased lands from Arab locals in the region, and companies such as "Zichron David" had been established in 1927 and in 1934. In exchange, the companies had promised that schools would be built in the villages. Attempts to establish a real settlement failed. However, the lands that had been purchased remained in Jewish hands.

The local population had been hostile to Jews for many generations. The Arabs had, in various ways, always attempted to make difficulties for Jews trying to settle in the mountains surrounding Jerusalem. However, the founders of the Settlement, such as Ben Gurion and Mr. Weitz had a dream and had the means to fulfill it. They understood, even then, the strategic importance of surrounding Jerusalem with Jewish settlements in order to control the main arteries leading to the entrance of Jerusalem. It goes without saying that this would be a difficult task from the aspect of

168 | THE POWER OF LIFE

economics and survival. It was very difficult to cultivate the land without sources of water. There were only a few small wells in the region that collected water during the winter, but of course, this would not be sufficient to carry out any substantial irrigation.

Nevertheless, there were "pioneers" who were ready to face this challenge and to sacrifice themselves selflessly in order to attain this sacred goal.

The first nucleus to go to "Kfar Etzion" had been organized in Lvov (Lemberg) in Galicia, not far from Buczacz, the city of my birth. As I stated earlier, my late brother, Lonek had studied at the university in Lvov and had described the city in his letters. The Ukraine, a country famous for pogroms, had given birth to many Zionist groups that concentrated on preparing themselves for emigration to the Land of Israel. It is very possible that there was a definite connection between the anti-Semitic nature of the country and the number of Zionists that originated from the Ukraine.

The British published the infamous "Land Laws" in 1940, forbidding Jews from acquiring and land within the borders of Palestine, including areas such as Hebron, Bethlehem and the surroundings of Jerusalem.

Nevertheless, the Jewish National Fund made significant efforts to purchase land, even in the forbidden regions. The Religious Kibbutz and the "Hashomer Hatza'ir" Movements took part in these efforts and decided to settle the region. Thus, during the early 1940's, three kibbutzim were established by the Religious Kibbutz Movement – first "Kfar Etzion", then "Massuot Yitzhak" and then "'Ein Tzurim". The "Hashomer Hatza'ir" Movement established Kibbutz "Revadim".

The region called "Gush Etzion", located equidistant from Jerusalem, the holy city, and from Hebron, the city of our forefathers, could be called the cradle of the nation. The area had been witness to many historical events that tied the people to the land.

It was from here that Abraham and Isaac walked for three days to Mt. Moriah, where Abraham planned to sacrifice his son.

It was at the foot of this mountain that Abraham made a covenant with God.

The first purchase of land in the Land of Israel was when Abraham purchased the Machpelah Cave and the adjoining field.

The Tribe of Judah settled in this region and took possession of it.

Farmers and vintners remained on the mountain, even after the expulsion of Jews from Judea and the destruction of the First Temple. There has always been continuous Jewish presence on Mt. Hebron, long after the expulsion of the ten tribes.

In this region, one can find Arab settlements that bear names that sound almost Jewish. These are mispronunciation of names which had been given to the cities belonging to the tribe of Judah. Archeological excavations in the region have exposed ancient relics bearing witness to a flourishing Jewish presence during different periods in history.

We reached "Massuot Yitzhak" by early evening. The kibbutz was located "between mountains and rocks." The landscape was simply remarkable. We could see some Arab villages in the distance. The perimeter of the kibbutz was lit up and it was surrounded by a barbed wire fence, a rather unpleasant reminder, for me and my friends, of other places and memories.

We knew that the region was not very friendly and that previous attempts to settle there had failed because of the difficulties involved in adapting to a mountainous region that lacked water and sources of income. In addition, the Arabs of the region would often attack the Jewish settlers. The kibbutz had a number of small stone houses, and several huts. The members of the kibbutz received us very warmly. We put our meager belongings in rooms that they had set up for us and went to the dining room, which had been decorated in our honor. After a rich meal, the kibbutz secretary greeted us and commended our intentions to join the kibbutz, thus, joining the Zionism Settlement Enterprise.

The next morning, we were taken to the clothing stores where we were given work clothes and then taken straight to the "work roster". I had been assigned to the machine that crushed rocks and stones, which were not lacking in this region, into gravel. This machine was called the "honey machine". We would throw the rocks into the machine and two thick metal plates would crush and crumble them, making gravel.

The machine was powered by a small diesel motor which would start loudly when we cranked its handle, turning the torque. Once, when I was working there, something very unpleasant happened. While I was throwing rocks into the container, the sleeve of my shirt got caught in the machine. Luckily, I was strong and was alert enough to quickly pull my arm out of the sleeve, which ended up being "chewed up and swallowed" by the machine. The thought of my arms going through this made me shiver in horror, and still does. This frightening incident taught me a lesson – I could have lost an arm so easily – I learned to be extra careful.

Several days later, I was assigned to a different work roster – I was told to harness a mule to a metal sled and haul away the rocks that were left in the field after boulders had been blown up, so that the land could be prepared for plowing. We rolled and carried tons of rocks, slowly preparing the land, inch by inch, for a field of potatoes. We used the stones to build terraces on the mountain slopes, as did the Arab farmers in the region, creating a small plot of land suitable for agriculture. The mule was very wild and not everyone was able to control it – he would jump and kick and refuse to budge, as mules are prone to do. My own experience with animals, dating back to my days in Europe, helped me control him.

After a hard day's work, we returned to the kibbutz. I would go straight to the dining room. There the tables were ready for us, with sliced bread, watered down jam (in order to make it go further) and tea without sugar. I would sit down and eat. The fresh air had made me very hungry and I could put away 12 slices of bread at a time (I was very thin at the time). To me, the bread tasted like heaven. This was true pioneering work: blowing up boulders, preparing terraces for planting, creating arable land (almost like making something out of nothing!). I was very proud of our work!

From the dining room, I would go to my room, covered with white dust from the rocks. I would take a towel and go to the public shower – the water was cold, but that didn't make me enjoy the shower any less.

Kibbutz "Massuot Yitzhak" was first established in 1942. The settlers were religious Jews from Czechoslovakia and Hungary, as well as some people who had been born in the country. They were real pioneers and served as wonderful examples to us. We saw people who were willing to devote themselves completely in order to establish a developed and well-grounded economy. We drew encouragement from them and put our own shoulders to the yoke.

The work in the kibbutz was difficult but we did it diligently and with dedication. There was a cowshed with cows, and a few henhouses. We found out for ourselves how difficult it was to make a living from agriculture in this area and how much of a lack of water there actually was.

During our leisure time, there were various activities available to us and each of us chose what interested him or her. Most took part in Gemara and Talmud lessons.

Our group arrived in Gush Etzion in 1947, a critical time in the fight for independence. The prevailing atmosphere in the country was tense and we felt this tension even more, being as we were, surrounded by hostile Arab villages. Immediately upon my arrival to "Massuot", I was inducted into the kibbutz Palmach unit (local units). We began training with a vengeance. I received an old, heavy Canadian rifle that I came to like very much. Its aim was very accurate. I also received overalls and high crepe-soled shoes, and there I was, a soldier. I was the youngest of the group and the auxiliary policeman's coat was too big for me. It resembled the uniform of the British police and I felt very important.

We trained very intensively. We would go into the mountains and approach the Arab villages that were notorious for their participation in the riots of 1929. Our instructors placed great emphasis on night exercises. It was very important to be familiar with all of the paths and be well conversant with the wadis and accesses to the Arab villages. This was because revenge operations had been planned for any village which would stage attacks on "Massuot Yitzhak" or on any person working the land around the settlement. The instructors would take us to places that were several kilometers away from the kibbutz and one by one, alone, we had to return to the meeting place. We walked in the moonlight and, of course, used the North Star and the big dipper as references. We crossed fields and mountains, climbed, slid, crawled. It was a difficult road, full of obstacles – rocks, stones, plants that would scratch and scrape the legs, etc. But we would let nothing stand in our way.

In Gush Etzion, November 1947

My squad leader was Zeev Yehudai and the district commander was Mussa Yakobovitch. Mussa would suddenly appear during the exercises, take a Sten submachine gun and fire live bullets at our feet while we were attacking. During breaks in training, I practiced firing at bottles until I became a sharpshooter.

Our squad was supposed to move about the Gush, sent wherever it was necessary to arrive quickly and return enemy fire. We were given the role of reinforcing the active forces, and whenever necessary, set up roadblocks. Our training was difficult and we took it very seriously. The aim was to build a small force, as well-trained as possible, able to return fire rapidly and accurately.

On November 29, 1947, we listened attentively to the radio, to the direct broadcast from New York from the U.N. building. The United Nations was voting on the decision to establish a Jewish state. We shouted with joy every time a country voted "yes" and complained with every "no". At the end, the vote was in favor of the establishment of a Jewish State. Along with the rest of the Settlement in the State of Israel, we rejoiced at the results. We danced and sang until dawn. The fact that according to the U.N. recommendation, Gush Etzion was supposed to remain in Arab hands did not cloud our joy that night. It was only the next day that we began to worry about the future.

The Battle of Gush Etzion

The day after the declaration of the State, the Arabs set up roadblocks on the road leading from Jerusalem to Gush Etzion and we were very quickly cut off, totally cut off, from the rest of the country. We were surrounded only by mountains, unable to be reached by vehicle. We were fully under siege, all supply routes cut off. Rumors reached us, via a British police officer from Hebron, that plans were underway to attack the Gush.

Nevertheless, we tried to carry on with our lives as normally as possible.

One day, I rode out to the fields carrying my rifle, an Arab plow attached to the horse's neck. I began plowing the ground, completely exposed to the mountains across from me, close to an Arab village. I had only managed to plow a few furrows when suddenly I heard a shot and a single bullet flew by me, followed by rifle fire coming at me from all directions. I quickly grabbed the horse and the plow and took them down to the foot of the mountain, where I took up a position and fired a few rounds in the direction from which the firing had come. Then I got on the horse, hung the plow around its neck again and returned to the kibbutz at a gallop. This was the "opening shot". That was how War of Independence began for me.

We quickly began digging trenches around the kibbutz and preparing positions to cover all approaches to the kibbutz, from all sides. In addition, we began to post nightly guard watches. We worked during the day and at night, we took turn standing guard for a few hours. Each of us, in turn, manned a guard position alone.

Gush Etzion was located in a mountainous and quite isolated region. There were no vehicles on the roads because the Arabs had blocked them. It was very quiet. Sometimes, you would hear a stone tumbling down the hill, and then you immediately became wary, turning to look in the direction of the noise, listening – what and who had made that noise? After a few minutes of tension, it would turn out to have been a rabbit who had shifted a rock when hopping, causing it to roll down and make the noise which had aroused such suspicion. Then the night would become quiet again and one could even hear the humming of a fly.

The winter nights were particularly difficult, especially when it rained constantly and one would be standing in a heavy British army coat, which weighed a ton when it was wet, so that, in addition to the rifle, one would be carrying a heavy load. However, I felt a sense of mission and it all seemed very natural to me.

Once in a while, our squad would be ordered to block Arab traffic between Hebron and Jerusalem. When we knew that a supply convoy was due to come to the Gush, we had to make sure that the road was blocked to Arabs so that it would remain open for the convoy to pass. We also did this when we received information that forces belonging to the Jordan Arab Legion were going to be sent in the direction of Jerusalem in order to attack Ramat Rachel. We mined the bridges at the crossroads and blew them up, and we even fought the Legion.

Occasionally, the Legion and Arab gangs would attack under the sponsorship of the British. To a certain extent, this might have been a way "to sounding us out", check out our capabilities. We had the upper hand during all of these skirmishes, causing the Arabs quite a few losses. Usually, they would retreat whenever we returned heavy fire.

One day, we were ordered to go down to the Jerusalem-Hebron road and set up a roadblock. We positioned ourselves in a trench close to the road, in one of the curves. We opened fire on every vehicle that appeared, causing it to retreat. We lay there for a full day and were only ordered to return to the kibbutz at sunset.

The next morning, carrying my rifle on my shoulder, I went out in a field that was about three kilometers away from the kibbutz to harvest some clover with the scythe. I had just begun to cut the clover when I suddenly heard shots from the direction of Kfar Etzion. I quickly ran in the direction of Massuot Yitzhak and when I arrived there, I was ordered to take the two-inch mortar. Nathan was my number two and he carried the shells. We ran in a crouch until we reached Kfar Etzion, where we reported to the district commander who ordered us to go to the western fence of the kibbutz. The rest of the combatants took up positions at all of the Gush's access points.

On the ridge facing us, approximately 200 meters as the crow flies, stood English armored vehicles, pouring fire onto Kfar Etzion. I immediately took up my position, calculated the firing angle based on distance and trajectory, aimed and fired a few shells. The fourth shell hit an armored vehicle, where a blond head was peering out, probably an Englishman. The firing stopped immediately. Apparently one of the attackers had been injured by shrapnel and they forces began retreating.

The British were helping the Arabs in their battles against us. They believed that the Jewish Settlement would not be able to survive. To this day, I find it difficult to explain why I was not afraid when I stood, coolly and fearlessly, facing the rifle fire that rained down on us, calmly finding a good position to fire the mortar shells.

Fortunately, we did not suffer any casualties from this attack.

A renewed attempt to bring us reinforcements and supplies was unsuccessful. In January 1948, we received a helium (sun) signal message from Ma'aleh Hahamisha that 35 people, under the command of Danny Maas, had left Hartuv carrying weapons and ammunition, and they were on their way to reinforce the Gush. They had left in the late afternoon and were due to arrive at dawn. When they failed to arrive, we began to get worried. We feared that something had happened to them along the way. At noon, our squad was ordered to advance in their direction, taking the path that they would have had to take. We went through wadis and passed very close to villages, looking for them everywhere, but did not find any signs of life. We returned to the kibbutz in the evening with heavy hearts. Later on, we were informed that they had all been killed in battle.

The next day, on January 17, 1948, the British brought their bodies in bags and unloaded them from the trucks. I was present at the time. These weren't bodies. They were human body parts that had been brutally savaged, as if by animals. The ears, nose and hands, as well as the men's sexual organs had been cut off each body and thrown to the dogs. I will never be able to forget this scene.

We later found out the whole story: The reinforcements consisted of 35 students from the Hebrew University of Jerusalem that had tried to reach Gush Etzion by going through wadis and Arab villages. They had planned to go through the wadis in order to avoid detection. Unfortunately, just before dawn, they came across an Arab shepherd tending his sheep. Instead of taking him captive or killing him, they decided to let him go, even though they knew that he had seen them. Their sensitive feelings sealed their fate. The shepherd ran to the nearest village shouting: "There are Jews in the wadi!" The villagers grabbed their weapons and ran to the deep wadi, where they killed all 35 fighters, one after the other, after a long and difficult battle. Then they mutilated them.

We buried the crushed bodies in a common grave in Gush Etzion. After the Six Days' War, after the liberation of the Gush, the remains of the 35 fighters were transferred for burial in the military cemetery in Mt. Herzl, together with the other victims of Gush Etzion.

We prepared a small airfield in the center of the Gush, so that piper cubs could land there. One day, we were surprised by a visit from a very honored guest – Yigal Alon, the legendary Palmach commander. He was making lightning visits to all of the settlements of the Gush, including us. We sat with him in the dining room and he brought us up to date on the situation on the different fronts, explaining how our people were dealing with attacks in all corners of the country.

We complained that we didn't have enough arms and ammunition and that we particularly lacked heavy machine-guns. We only had light machine-guns, like an Italian "Breda", which would jam after every other burst. Alon promised that a supply convoy would be sent to us very soon – he couldn't promise weapons, telling us plainly that there was a great lack of weapons all over the country and that we would have to make do with what we had. Our mission was to stop the Arab Legion at any cost, because our positions were the first line of fighting to prevent the Legion from reaching Jerusalem.

We got the message and were determined to fulfill

the assignments given us. This was despite the fact that we knew that it would be almost impossible to stand our ground if the hordes of Arabs decided to attack us en masse.

As a man and as a commander, Yigal Alon was very impressive. He inspired us all with confidence. We were all willing to follow such a man, even knowing the danger involved. The War of Independence was marked with the bravery of its commanders and fighters on all fronts.

And so we lived, worked, guarded, fought. Food was doled out in small portions because we had very little of it. We were never really hungry, although we learned to be satisfied with very little. Our reward was that we were able to breathe clear, clean mountain air every day.

Some time later, at the end of March, we received the news that a supply convoy was on its way to us and we were told to make every effort to enable it to reach us. We had to completely block all Arab movement on the Hebron-Jerusalem road. At approximately 10:00 a.m. we heard the noise of vehicles traveling in the direction of the Gush. Dozens of vehicles arrived: busses, armored vehicles and trucks, all laden with all sorts of supplies for the whole Gush. It was very important to unload them quickly, so that they could immediately return to Jerusalem before the Arabs managed to block the road. These same trucks plied the Tel Aviv-Jerusalem line, bringing food to Jerusalem, thus enabling the city to hold out. The commanders of the convoy were in a hurry to return because there was a chance that in the meantime, the Arab gangs would manage to block the road with rocks, making it the convoy an easy target for an ambush.

Unfortunately, this is exactly happened.

Just before dawn the next morning, a soldier arrived, wounded in the leg. He had been part of the convoy. He had made his way back to us under the cover of the night. He told us all the details of the battle that had taken place when the convoy was attacked. I knew him. His name was Pinkus and he had studied in "Mikveh Yisrael" while I had been there.

It was very hard to listen to a description of the battle. The Arabs had blocked the roads in many places. When the vehicles of the supply convoy reached the bend in the road near Solomon's Pools, the Arabs had already placed mounds of rocks on the road. As the first truck reached the roadblock, the Arabs opened fire on the truck and the truck driver was seriously wounded. After successfully maneuvering around a few of rocks, the convoy finally had to come to a stop. The Arabs began firing on the trapped trucks from all directions. They killed many of the people who had found refuge in a building in Neve Daniel next to the road.

We later found out that despite the difficult situation, some of the trucks had managed to break through the roadblocks and had reached the Bethlehem police post. The British refused to go to the battle area and rescue the wounded and the dead. It was only the next day that the British did this, and then, it goes without saying that no one was left alive. The bodies bore signs of savage abuse.

This was a very sad day for the residents of Jerusalem, who had waited in vain for the men and vehicles that were supposed to be bringing supplies to the city.

We became very depressed when we found out that so many members of the convoy, which later became known as the "Bnei Daniel Convoy", had been killed. We also realized that convoys would no longer be able to reach the Gush.

There weren't many soldiers remaining from the "Palmach" division in Gush Etzion. They were scattered from Kfar Etzion to the Russian monastery, and during Arab attacks, we would fight side by side with them.

The members of the "Palmach" were wonderful people. I wanted to be like them, with their free behavior, the bravery they displayed and their ability to go to battle calmly, ready for any sacrifice, determined and relentless. There have been many stories told about the operations of the "Palmach", but not enough. In fact, it was the "Palmach" that saved Jerusalem. The "Harel" Brigade, commanded by the late Yitzhak Rabin, directed the battles on the road to Jerusalem and guarded the convoys that brought food supplies to Jerusalem. Today, on the road leading to Jerusalem, one can still see, lying by the roadside, burnt remnants of the armored cars that brought supplies to Jerusalem. The road was very narrow and Arab gangs would ambush the convoys from the hills along the road.

Many fell here, giving their lives in the defense of Jerusalem. The battle continued until we were victorious, and "hungry" Jerusalem was saved.

The members of the Palmach were the real heroes of the War of Independence.

Gush Etzion had only about 300 combatants – men and women. I must emphasize that the women showed extraordinary courage, both as fighters and when they were taking care of the wounded. There was no question of sexism when it came to fighting for one's country and one existence.

The siege was complete and when we saw that we were completely cut off, we took stock of the situation. We felt that we had had no choice. We had to fight with everything we had and prepare ourselves for a battle to the death – there would be no opportunity to retreat. We were on a small island, surrounded by Arab villages. Nevertheless, our spirits remained high and we did not despair.

On May 12, 1948, the Arabs launched a deadly and final assault on Gush Etzion. The Jordanian Legion led the attack with 45 armored cars and were followed by tens of thousands of villagers who covered the mountains, turning the surrounding mountains black with their dark robes.

As the attack began, our squad was ordered to run and take a position on a rocky hill in the middle of the Gush. This hill commanded a view of the entrance to the Gush, particularly the access to Kfar Etzion. My classmate Shimon and I took up the furthest position, the one that was closest to the road, overlooking the whole area of the entrance. The "Russian Monastery" was on our right, close to the Hebron road, manned by members of the Armored Corps who had succeeded in arriving from Tel Aviv to provide reinforcements in the Gush. After a few hours of very intense fighting, the Jordanian soldiers succeeded in storming the "Russian Monastery", where a hand-to-hand battle took place as our people fell back, forced to give up position after position. Many of our combatants fell there, among them the poet Zvi ben Yosef, author of the poem "Yesh li Kinneret" ("I have a Kinneret", about the beauty of the Sea of Galilee). He caught a burst of machine gun fire and died on the spot. The story goes that his last words were: "If I forget thee, O Jerusalem, may my right hand forget its cunning." The fall of the monastery into Arab hands gave them a strategic advantage. The "Yellow Hill" on our right remained in our hands, overlooking the access road to the Gush, where it split in the direction of Kfar Etzion and Massuot Yitzhak, Ein Tzurim and Revadim. All of the heavy fire was concentrated on the Yellow Hill and towards us, on the rocky hill.

After a day of heavy fighting, we were ordered to come to Kfar Etzion to transfer all of the wounded from there to Massuot Yitzhak because we realized that the Arab Legion intended to first conquer the Kfar, which served as a symbol of the Gush. The squad regrouped in a line in the rear and I was ordered to be the scout and lead the column to Kfar Etzion. I went ahead, making sure that I did not make the slightest noise. I crept forward and suddenly saw someone lying on the ground. I signaled the squad to halt, approached the body, and saw that it was one of our fighters, who had been killed at the entrance to the Kfar.

We entered Kfar Etzion and began dealing with the convoy of wounded, where we found that some had been seriously wounded and would have to be transported on stretchers. Those who were slightly wounded, walked. Avrasha Tamir (later to become a general in the IDF) was one of the wounded, suffering from shell shrapnel all over his body. After the wounded had been placed on stretchers, we began going back in the direction of Massuot Yitzhak, with me leading the convoy via a path with which I was very familiar. While walking, from about 50 meters away, we heard the voices of Arabs. We were very careful, but at that time, the Arabs did not fight at night. Thus we reached Massuot Yitzhak, taking turns carrying the seriously wounded. The nurses and the medics were waiting for us there. The wounded were put into a house that had been turned into a temporary hospital.

We were ordered to go back and once again take up our position on the rocky hill, in an attempt to slow down the advance of the Jordanian Legion and the Arab gangs.

The battle was renewed at dawn and the "Yellow Hill" fell. Its defenders were unable to withstand the larger forces and the heavy fire that rained down upon them. They had probably also run out of ammunition.

The fighters who were left withdrew to Massuot
Yitzhak. After the "Yellow Hill" had been captured, all
of the firepower was concentrated upon us. In fact, we
were the last line of defense before the entrance to Kfar
Etzion. Suddenly, I saw a convoy of about 40 armored
cars advancing from one side, and from the other, from
the hill on the right, from the direction of the Russian
Monastery, I could see soldiers of the Legion forming
a long line, getting ready to attack. This was a sure sign
that the attack was about to take place. It is difficult to
describe this sight. Immense forces moving towards
you and you lying facing them from a small position,
with very little ammunition. I had a few armor piercing
shells and when the first armored car began making the
turn in the road towards the entrance to Kfar Etzion, I
hit its front tire and it stopped in its tracks, blocking the
turn and because there were large boulders on either
side of the road, no other vehicle could go around it.
The convoy had come to a stop. In the meantime, the
infantry had advanced to a distance of 20 meters from
us, stopping just below the rocky hillside upon which
we lay. I immediately threw two grenades in their
direction. Apparently many of them were either
wounded or killed. They began to retreat and Shimon
and I fired at them, over and over, until the rifle became
too hot to hold. In order to prevent blisters, I held it
with my "stocking cap" and kept firing, until I ran out
of bullets.

For me, who had been the victim of persecution and
had experienced so much danger in my life and who

had fought so hard to survive, there was special significance to the battle for Gush Etzion. I knew that I was fighting for a holy cause, not just for my own life.

One of the wonderful things about human nature is that during moments of the greatest danger, one doesn't think of the fact that he/she may die, but rather how to destroy the enemy, staying calm and not going into a panic.

During difficult moments in a battle, when shells are exploding on large boulders and thousands of bullets are being directed at a person, only one thought crosses one's mind: "jealousy" that the enemy has unlimited ammunition and you can only fire a few shells.

Attempts were made to reach us from the direction of Massuot Yitzhak and to bring us ammunition, and they did manage to get some bullets to us. However, within two hours, these too were gone. All of a sudden, a small Piper Cub appeared in the sky and tried to parachute some ammunition down to us. As soon as it appeared, fierce fire opened up on it from all directions and it was forced to remain at a high altitude, and when it finally dropped the parcel, it was blown towards the Arabs.

On the afternoon of May 13, 1948, when I had only one bullet left, we were ordered to fall back to Massuot Yitzhak. As you recall, we were at the top of a hill and from there, we had to go down a slope because the next kibbutz was lower. One of my friends, Eliezer, rose to his feet and was immediately greeted by a hail of bullets, which wounded him in the ear. I decided to roll down the hill, holding my rifle between my legs, just as we had been taught, and rolling, scratched and wounded, finally reached the bottom.

We reached the kibbutz, exhausted after two difficult days of fighting, suffering from lack of sleep because we had been awake for the past 48 hours. But there was no time to think about being tired. We were immediately sent to reinforce all the positions in the kibbutz and prepared ourselves for our last stand, our own "Massada". We knew that we had no other choice. Behind my position, I could hear the members of the kibbutz setting mines around the temporary hospital buildings, so that if, God forbid, we reached "our last moments", they would blow up the hospital buildings along with the wounded lying there so that they would not fall into the hands of the Arabs who would certainly torture and finish them off.

After we had left the rocky hill, the Arabs attacked in great numbers and stormed Kfar Etzion. Two wounded reached us in "Massuot", after having crawled the whole night. One of the wounded told us about the battle: at the beginning of the battle, the commander of the Gush, Mosh, who had been a great fighter and daring commander, a war hero, was one of the first to fall with the onslaught of the attack. Those who remained behind, mostly wounded people, decided that they would come out holding white flags as a sign of surrender and walk towards the soldiers of the Legion. But the legionnaires did not honor the white flags and butchered those holding them. The Arabs entered the kibbutz and went from house to house, from post to post. Hand-to-hand combat resulted and the remaining defenders were killed.

This story added force to our opinion that we would fight until the last bullet and would not give in. I, personally, was completely at peace with the thought that this may be the last battle of my life. At least I had fulfilled my dream and my teacher's testament by having reached Jerusalem and I had made my modest contribution to the establishment of the State of Israel.

Today, this probably sounds very trite, a cliché, but then I could only think of one phrase: "How good it is to die for one's country."

Our radio was not working because the batteries were dead. All we had left was signal communication with Kibbutz Ma'aleh HaHamisha. Using this method of communication, we were informed that negotiations were underway between Ben Gurion and King Abdullah of Jordan with regard to our becoming prisoners of the Jordanians. Our command level was against such a capitulation, particularly in view of what had happened in Kfar Etzion.

In the meantime, we continued our preparations for the last battle, feeling very depressed but fiercely determined to fight until the bitter end. It was very quiet outside, almost pastoral. No one panicked and we were prepared for any eventuality.

Captivity

On the afternoon of May 14, 1948, Ben Gurion ordered us to surrender and precise conditions were set as to how the Legion soldiers would enter our positions. It was decided that we would hand over our positions one at a time and that soldiers of the Legion would occupy each position, thereby forming a barrier between us and the unruly mob that had gathered all around and was shouting "butcher the Jews!" Suddenly, one of the officers of the Arab Legion, a captain, approached, accompanied by a few other officers. The captain, who was immaculately dressed in the best English tradition, informed us that he had received a direct order from King Abdullah of Jordan to protect us "as if we were his children" and gave us his word as an officer and a gentleman that nothing untoward would happen to us. We had no choice but to trust him.

We began collecting our weapons and stacking them into a pile. When we were finished, the captain came to us, threw an ingenious glance at the meager pile and said: "What? This is what you used to fight us? If I had only ten soldiers like you, I'd be in Tel Aviv tomorrow."

It was only when the Legion soldiers began to man our positions and without hesitation, began firing into the mob that we truly began believing that they would be able to keep their promise and that we might, after all, remain alive.

The villagers began looting the property. Our mules broke into a run, trying to get away. One of them was "my" mule. The Arab "heroes" tried to catch him, but to no avail. When he kicked left and right, I thought to myself: "Well, at least he's getting even with them." Only I knew how to control him.

In the meantime, trucks had approached and we climbed into them in an orderly fashion. The wounded and the women were taken to Bethlehem under heavy guard. It was after midnight by the time the convoy was ready to set out. This was Friday, May 15, 1948. In Tel Aviv, just a short time before, Ben Gurion had officially declared the establishment of the State of Israel. We were unaware of this in "real time" but only found out about it much later. Ben Gurion said "…We hereby declare the establishment of a Jewish state in Eretz-Israel, to be known as the State of Israel…" just as we were on our way to Hebron as prisoners.

When our guards boarded the trucks, I felt a shock: I saw two blond men speaking German to each other. The din and noise of the truck prevented me from hearing what they were saying. I knew that there were all kinds of mercenaries fighting on the side of the Arabs, but it never occurred to me that there would be Germans among them. I couldn't help thinking of the possibility, the real possibility, that during the Second World War, they had been soldiers in the German army and might very well have taken part in anti-Jewish activities. Fate indeed mocks people.

Those were very difficult moments for me: once again, I was trapped, unable to protect myself, and being led to prison or a prison camp under guard. Me? I had always been able to escape before when I found myself in danger. Old habits made me prepare my body for some action. I considered trying to jump out of the truck, but I couldn't. I was with my group and I couldn't just abandon them. I felt I had to stay with them… The thought that I was not alone calmed me down a little.

It wasn't long before we reached the prison in Hebron, the city of the patriarchs. I figured that the Machpelah Cave, the burial place of Abraham, Isaac and Jacob, was not too far away. We got off the trucks and entered the prison in an orderly fashion. The prison was an old fortress, dating back to the Turks, possibly even older. I was very unhappy because I had left my "lucky charm", my piece of shrapnel, back in Massuot Yitzhak. I had been afraid to take it with me because I didn't want to get into any trouble with the soldiers of the Legion. I hoped against all hope that I would be able to see it again, one of these days.

We were put into small cells. It was very crowded; there simply was not enough room for so many prisoners. During the time that we were getting organized in the cells and during the resulting confusion, we suddenly heard terrible screams from behind the cells. The doctor of the Gush had suddenly gone mad, taken off all his clothes and begun running round and round. The guards took the prisoners out of his cell and left him there alone. The doctor continued to run wild until they finally succeeded in calming him down. They divided the people taken from his cell between the other cells, making them even more overcrowded.

The lot of the prisoners was uncertainty. We did not really sleep that night. People talked among themselves and each one tried to imagine where they would take us, to what prisoners' camp and where. For me, these hours were very difficult. Once again I had that familiar feeling of helplessness that one gets when one is cornered and sees no escape. After all, here I was, the escape master, even while being shot at with a machine gun, even when dozens of Germans and Ukrainians aimed their rifles at me, chasing me on foot and on horseback, even after they had caught me. They had tried to kill me several times, and I had always managed to escape and survive.

The whole time that we were in the prison, I stayed close to my friend, Shimon Markovitch, who was a few years older than me. We had fought together, shoulder to shoulder, on the rocky hill. And now, we were standing in a small cell, looking around. The thick walls were like the walls of a fortress, impossible to breach. We cheered each other up and hoped that we would manage, one way or another, to get out of this trap.

With dawn, on that same terrible Shabbat, a mob of people from the villages began gathering around the prison, armed with daggers and knives, and shouting, "death to the Jews!" The atmosphere was very unpleasant – the Legion soldiers were guarding us, but we didn't know if they could do anything in the face of these thousands of rioters. Several of the prisoners, ignoring what was going on outside, began reciting the Psalms and other prayers. I didn't feel that I could put my trust in the Master of the Universe and said to my friend, Shimon Markovitch: "Let's grab a rifle from one of the Legion soldiers and try to shoot into the mob." Just then, the captain who had been in charge of our capture appeared and alighting from his jeep, ordered the soldiers of the Legion open fire on the crowd and disperse it. We couldn't believe our eyes, but it was true. The shots scared the crowd and the people retreated from the prison very quickly. It was only then that we truly believed that King Abdullah had really decreed that they were to protect us, and this eased our worries.

After beginning to feel some hope regarding our future, we relaxed somewhat from the recent events. This was Saturday morning and it was time for the morning prayers. Most of the group prayed assiduously. Shimon Markovitch and I did not participate in the prayers. We stood in a corner of the prison, and from there we could see the main entrance to the prison. Suddenly we noticed a whole delegation of high-ranking officers, even a colonel, in dress uniforms. We later found out that these were Egyptian officers and that the Egyptian army had managed to invade the country and to reach Beersheba and its surroundings. We understood that the Iraqi army had also invaded the country through Jordan and had reached the West Bank of the Jordan River. This news did not exactly gladden our hearts.

The Egyptian soldiers, accompanied by British army officers commanding King Abdullah's Legion, had come to see the prisoners. John Bagot Glubb, who had changed his name to Glubb Pasha (in Arabic) was the commanding officer of the Legion. All of the units were commanded by British officers and the weapons and ammunition came from British armories.

This presented a complete picture of the British "gentlemen". Until 15 May 1948, they had helped the Arabs attack the Jews, searched Jewish settlements for weapons, and if any was found, they had confiscated the arms, thereby not allowing the Jews to defend themselves. Often, they would turn around and sell those same weapons to the Arabs, in return for a few bottles of whiskey. After the declaration of independence, they helped the Arabs in other ways.

During my stay in prison, I wondered, afraid, if the small Jewish Settlement in the Land of Israel would succeed in repelling all of the armed and organized Arab armies, since all we had were very few weapons, not enough ammunition and only a handful of combatants.

We passed another difficult night. The next morning, on Sunday, we heard the sound of trucks outside and were told that we were about to be transported to Jordan. We got on the trucks in an orderly fashion, 40 to each truck, sitting in rows with the guards sitting on the roofs of the trucks, both to make sure that we didn't escape and that no harm would come to us on the way. That was the beginning of our journey to Jordan, where in every village, large crowds lined the road to catch a glimpse of us, spitting, shouting and cursing us. Someone had apparently taken the time to tell them that this was a convoy of Jewish prisoners. A particularly large crowd filled the streets when we passed through Jericho, a miserable, filthy city, its streets crying out with poverty. We traveled quite fast. We crossed the Allenby Bridge and continued to Rabat Amon. The city sits on hills and the view from there was quite spectacular. It resembled what Petach Tikva looked like later in the 1950's.

We passed through Rabat Amon quickly and as darkness fell, we reached a distant place in the desert called Mafrak, situated on the road leading from Jordan to Iraq. A few kilometers past Mafrak, we stopped at out destination, Camp "Omel-Jemal". It was in the middle of the desert, surrounded by wilderness. We could see the indistinct shapes of buildings weakly lit up by kerosene lamps. We got off the trucks and approached the gate, which was very narrow. At the gate stood a very large sergeant major named Abu Yakub, who greeted every person entering the camp by hitting him on the back. This was the "reception" we were given. We began to get organized in the tents, 12 persons to a tent. We each received a blanket and lay down on the ground. Despite the fact that it wasn't comfortable, we fell asleep immediately.

When I got up in the morning, all I could see was

desert, desert on all sides. I squinted my eyes in an effort to see if there was any sign of life. Nothing. Only sand. After a few minutes of staring at the monotonous yellow sand, my senses began to reel. And then, for the very first time in my life, I witnessed a fata morgana. My visions seemed to be far away and the images changed – fruit-bearing trees, a stormy sea, houses with red-tile roofs, a horseman galloping on a horse, etc. I rubbed my eyes and told myself that this, after all, was only fata morgana and that I should return immediately to the reality around me, despite the feeling of magic that these images evoked in me.

After being woken up in the morning, we were called to the parade grounds, where we sat cross-legged and the sergeant counted us. This became our daily routine. We would sit like that every morning and the sergeant would count us, using his fingers. Every time he made a mistake, he would begin all over again. Since he often made mistakes, we would have to sit like that for hours, the sun beating down on us, our legs aching, completely silent.

We elected Yosef Blaustein as our commander, who had been captured before us, in the power plant in Naharayim, together with a group of engineers working there. We called him "Abu Yussuf". He was a personal friend of King Abdullah and spoke fluent Arabic. He was allowed walk around freely and could to go visit the Jordanian Legion officer who commanded the soldiers guarding us. Almost all of the soldiers were Bedouins, loyal to the king. The captain himself was

Circassian and he had a radio in his tent. When he was in the camp commander's tent, Abu Yussuf could listen to the radio, to the Israeli Kol Yisrael station, and he would hear what was happening in the country, on the battlefront. Someone was in charge in every tent and all of the tent heads would meet with Abu Yussuf in one of the tents and then pass on the latest news to us.

We had to be careful not to talk too much in the presence a group of ultra-religious Jews who belonged to the Naturei Karta, the ultra-ultra-religious sect who had been captured in the Old City, because they were anti Zionists and were opposed the establishment of the State of Israel. They had even organized a delegation to meet with King Abdullah in order to ask permission to return to live in the Old City, in the Arab Quarter, so that they would not have to live in a "Zionist" state … unfortunately, he refused them permission.

The days passed very, very slowly. When winter came, we dug deep trench inside the tent, a half a meter deep, so that the tent would be protected from the winds and make us feel more secure.

The camp guards were replaced every few months. One day, a fanatical soldier, apparently a Palestinian, approached the machine gun position in one of the corners of the camp. He fired a few rounds of the machine gun and some of our people were killed and others wounded. After that, we found out that his family had been killed during an Etzel operation in Dir Yassin. This incident created tension in the camp and a feeling of insecurity, but the Legion commander assured us that from then on, only loyal Bedouin soldiers would be our guards.

Water was kept in large containers placed in a corner of the camp. We would come with our mess kits and fill them with drinking water. In order to wash, we would fill a pail and one person would empty the pail into a small tin can over the head of the other, in an attempt to save water. Thus, at noon, it was possible to see a group of naked men standing, pouring small amounts of water over each other – this was the washing "ritual".

At the beginning of our incarceration, the food was very bad. Our breakfast only consisted of wormy biscuits and a triangle of cheese. Lunch was soup distributed in the camp square. The desert climate would often bring with it waves of sandstorms, so that we always had some sand in our soup. However, we found a solution – if we waited long enough, the sand would sink to the bottom of the bowl and then we could drink our soup. However we never found a solution for the sand and dust storms that came immediately after our showers. On the other hand, we found out that one can get used to anything and after a while, even the dust became a routine phenomenon.

When we began receiving wages from home, a few pounds a month, we pooled our money together and bought pitas and olives, greatly improving our food situation.

We organized all kinds of activities in the camp to help us while away the endless hours on our hands. I attended classes on history and on Jewish studies taught by a few professors from the Hebrew University in Jerusalem who had been captured in the Old City. We also carried out physical exercises next to the tents.

Our main entertainment was watching the Bedouin soldiers drill. They couldn't get used to wearing shoes and so they were barefoot during their parade drills. Each held an onion in one hand and a tomato in the other, and the commander would shout: "onion" "tomato" "onion" "tomato" — this was their "right" "left" "right" left". It took them a long time to understand the concept and until they did, this sight provided us with entertainment.

As Rosh Hashanah and Yom Kippur drew near, a choir was formed, led by a Cantor. It was a truly moving sight: Jews standing in the middle of the Arab desert, praying, singing bursting from the tent that served as a synagogue. This was an inspiring experience.

My companions would write and receive letters all the time – but I had no one to write to. I had lost contact with my sister. At the time, she was still in Italy, awaiting papers to be able to travel to the United States. She had no idea where I might be. Later on, she married and moved to the United States and contact between us was only renewed after I returned from captivity.

In the fall, a ceasefire was declared and there was talk about an exchange of prisoners. One fine day, we were informed that we would be exchanged. The exchange ratio was eight Jordanian soldiers for every Israeli soldier. We were happy to learn that we would be free very soon and were impatient for the day to come. We had been prisoners for 10 and a half months. It had seemed endless, partially because in the desert, days are long.

Our day of freedom had arrived. This was around March-April 1949. One evening, our commander told us to prepare ourselves, pack our belongings and be ready to move out the next day.

The Mikveh Yisrael group, after returning from the prison camp in Jordan, March 1949

Liberation

A convoy of trucks arrived at dawn and we began boarding the trucks, according to groups. We passed Mafrak, Zarqa, Rabat Amon and once again crossed the Allenby Bridge, this time going the other direction, traveling until we reached the Mandelbaum Gate in Jerusalem. We found it difficult to sort out the way we felt when we crossed the border to the Israeli side. Hundreds of people were waiting for us there, as well as representatives of the IDF (Israel Defense Forces). After hugging many people and going through the initial stages of being received, an IDF officer from army personnel, Simcha Biyamini, turned to me and said: "Did you know that you have relatives in Ramat Hasharon? Their name is Acker. The wife's maiden name was Anderman." Binyamini gave me their address and after a while, I contacted them. Mrs. Lina Acker was a relative of the Anderman family from Buczacz. I used to visit them once in a while and they were always nice to me.

In the meantime, they announced that all returned prisoners were to come to the main synagogue in Jerusalem for a party. Chief Rabbi Herzog greeted us, as well as the commander of Jerusalem, General Shaltiel. After the ceremony, we each went our own way. I went with our group to Abu Kabir in Tel Aviv, where members of Massuot Yitzhak were living in a few abandoned houses.

In the evening, they had a large party for us and we were reunited with the women and children of Massuot Yitzhak who had been evacuated before the fighting had begun in the Gush.

The next day, some of us went for a walk on Allenby Street until we came to the "Whitman" ice cream parlor. There we drank some gazoz and ate some ice cream. We walked to the beach, sat on the sand and simply enjoyed sitting in the sun and looking at the view. I felt relaxed and calm. I wondered – once again, I had been saved and managed to survive. I had won this battle too. That was a wonderful feeling.

After a few days of vacation, I began thinking about my future: What would I do? Where should I go? My friends from Massuot Yitzhak were planning to go and start a new kibbutz in the area of Kastina in the south (near Beer Tuvia), where they had received land from the Jewish National Fund. I wasn't too keen on the idea. I wanted to do something for my home, even though I didn't have one yet. I decided to study a profession that would help me get ahead in life and build my future. I had no one to talk to about this – and so I only consulted myself. After having made my decision, I went to the rehabilitation department of the Ministry of Defense, and they sent me to the central army workshop and auto repair shop in Bayit Va-gan, in Jerusalem. I met with the commander of the workshop and he accepted me as an apprentice in general mechanics. I would travel there every day from Tel Aviv. For the most part, the workshop overhauled six-wheeler trucks and command cars. They would dismantle everything: the engine, the transformer, the gear, the back axle, etc, and then replace the worn or damaged parts. I worked there conscientiously, learned fast and within a few months advanced very nicely, but I began to feel that this was not what I wanted to do with my life. The work bored me. It was very monotonous and repetitive. In the meantime, I had learned to drive a truck and acquired a driver's license.

In the evenings, I would meet friends in Tel Aviv and it was through them that I learned that my cousin Willi (Zeev) was living in the city. I looked him up and we fell in each other's arms. He was also wondering what to do. He found out that Mekorot Water was building large pumps in the Negev for the national water carrier, and it would be easy to get jobs there as truck drivers and earn some money. We purchased an old Chevrolet truck through an army tender, repaired it and equipped it with a dumper on the back. This took several months.

When the truck was finally ready, I took it out of the garage and, pleased with myself, sat behind the wheel. I was going to take my first trip in a vehicle that I owned. I drove through Petach Tikva, in the direction of Tel Aviv. Suddenly I heard a thump in the front of the truck. I immediately stopped and saw a young girl caught under the front wheels of the truck and badly hurt. She had been riding a bicycle very fast, without looking where she was going. I called an ambulance and the police came as well. The girl kept on shouting – "The driver isn't to blame! The driver isn't to blame!" The ambulance took her to the hospital. The police investigator examined the truck and declared it to be in good order. I went to visit the girl in the hospital several times. Luckily for her, and for me, she recovered from the accident.

For me, it had been a shock, and not a pleasant start to my new career.

A few days later, Willi and I went South, to a place near Kibbutz Shuval. We were immediately hired to remove dirt from the place where they were digging to build the underground water pumps. The days were hot, burning summer days. The motor of the truck was in the cut off cabin of the truck. The heat reached 60 degrees centigrade, but we continued working without stop. We loaded four and a half cubic feet of dirt on the single axle truck bed, Willi and I taking turns at the wheel.

We worked like this for a month, until, during one of the transports, I overloaded the truck and when I raised the dumper, the front of the truck went up in the air, like a wild horse. The truck overturned, with me in it. The dumper was dislodged and fell off and the chassis became bent. I got out of this without a scratch, but in the blink of an eye, our business venture had ended. We did not have comprehensive insurance or any money to invest in repairing the truck. In fact, we were still very deeply in debt. Despite all of these problems, we didn't allow ourselves to wallow in self-pity and recovered quickly. We decided to leave the truck were it was and traveled to Beersheba to look for work. This was in the beginning of 1950. At the time, only "Solel Boneh" was providing work. This was a large Histadrut company. We were both hired by the company – at first I worked in the main building, in the warehouse that contained materials and Zeev became a work supervisor for a company that was paving the Sodom-Eilat road. We were given a room in Beersheba but on weekends, we lived together in Tel Aviv, on Rothschild Blvd, in a small apartment belonging to my cousin.

At that time, Beersheba was just a small speck in the desert. Solel Boneh had just begun building the first houses there. I was put in charge of a group of fifty Bedouins and my assignment was to supervise the loading of sand from the wadis onto the trucks, and make sure they were brought to where the cement was being mixed. Wadi sand was considered to be excellent for making concrete because it was mixed with small stones that added in addition to gravel. This mixture made the cement very strong.

When the trucks reached the wadi, I would line the Bedouins up on both sides of the truck, and then all one could see were shovels throwing sand into the truck. It was like a symphony - the sand flying through the air and landing in the truck. It would only take fifteen minutes to fill the truck. I supplied sand to a number of building sites.

I had a jeep at my disposal and could drive it anytime and anywhere I wanted. I took a real interest in the work. I felt that I was contributing to the building of the country.

Every Friday, the Sheikh of the local Beduin tribe that supplied the workers, would invite me to join him for a hafla (a feast). We would sit on the floor of the tent, around trays loaded with mutton, rice and many hardboiled eggs. I would eat 8 or 10 eggs at a time! At the time I didn't know that this wasn't healthy, thank God – nothing untoward has happened to me as a result of this "gluttony". Friday afternoon, I would go to Tel Aviv to spend the weekend with my friends. I would meet my cousin Willi at the apartment. He had also come to Tel Aviv to spend the weekend, I would take a cold shower because there usually wasn't any hot water, but I was used to that. We would put on our Shabbat clothes, walk down Allenby in the direction of the sea, where we would meet our friends in the "Martef Habira" (the Beer Cellar) coffee shop. This place was famous for its good beer and humus with black pepper. We exchanged stories about what we had done during the week.

On one of these Saturdays, while walking down Allenby, I met Dov Landau, a friend of mine. He had a girlfriend called Shoshana, whom he later married. We agreed to meet the following Saturday and they brought another girl, a friend of theirs named Chava, to the meeting. We went to the movies and had a good time, and that is how I came to meet my future wife. It is difficult to believe that 50 years have passed since that day.

On Sunday, we would return to Beersheba and go

back to work. This was a time that many new immigrants began arriving in Beersheba and neighborhoods sprang up like mushrooms after the rain. A number of Moshavim were established around the city. I would go to work in the morning, at dawn, and return in the evening, covered with dust from head to toe, with the exception of my eyes, which were hidden behind goggles to protect them from the sand and the dust. I did all of my traveling on dirt roads, which, in the winter, would turn into quagmires, trapping many vehicles.

One day, I was told that Golda Meir (then the Minister of Labor) would be coming to see us and that I had been assigned to take her to visit the Dead Sea, Mizpe Ramon, Yeruham and the Small and Large Craters. Meetings had been set up for her with the persons who were in charge on all of these sites.

I was very pleased with the honor I was accorded. We began driving in an open jeep, a 1942 model, part of the surplus equipment that the British army had left behind. Golda climbed in the jeep, put a kerchief over her head and off we went. We spoke the whole way. She was interested in where I had come from and when I had immigrated to Israel. I told her a bit about myself and in a nutshell, what I had gone through during the war. I noted that her eyes filled with tears. I also mentioned what I had done in Gush Etzion. She was very excited. "Such a young man, with such a rich past."

We discussed the plans that she had for the Dead Sea

and the rest of the places we visited, such as Dimona and Yerucham, which, at the time, were only pinpoints on the map, without any inhabitants. Her words made a deep impression on me. After all, there was only desert here, desolation, and no sea. How could anyone build a life here?

At that time, the roads in the Negev were very narrow and full of potholes. We reached the "scorpion's road" (a very steep and winding road leading from the Negev to Arad) and on one of the curves, where there was only room for one vehicle, I found myself face to face with a truck. I reversed and moved over, going over a rock, off the road, just at the edge of the mountain. Golda was not afraid and didn't say a word.

We returned to the hotel in Beersheba in the evening. It had formerly been an Arab house, with only a few miserable rooms. Golda took a cold shower, because there was no hot water. At 18:00, she came down from her room and ordered a glass of tea. In the meantime, a number people began arriving for a meeting - representatives from the Ministry of Finance, the Ministry of Commerce and Industry, as well as from the Ministry of Agriculture. All of a sudden, I caught sight of a friend of mine from my "Mikveh Yisrael" days. "Nathan", I said, "What are you doing here?" He told me that he had come to instruct new immigrants living in the Moshavim. "But there's no water and the houses haven't been constructed yet!" I said. He replied, with a smile: "If you will it, it is no fairy tale." Yes, that's the way it worked in those days – it was all founded on visions, faith and a lot, a lot of hope. In those days, people tended to act more and talk less!

That year, it was decided that construction would begin on the Dead Sea Works, and the next day, the papers cried "Golda intends to bury 10 million dollars in the Dead Sea!" – but this didn't scare Golda and she built that plant, and the "Dead" Sea has brought life to the whole Negev, particularly to Beersheba and to Arad. It is thanks to this plant, which exports billions of dollars worth of chemicals every year, and thanks to the work of others, that we were able to populate the Negev and turn it into the flourishing garden that it is today.

I am still proud of the minor role I played in the history of this pioneering period. We would work 12-14 hours a day, without receiving any pay for overtime. There was an feeling of dedication, of being on a mission, and everybody was just swept along with it. The prevalent feeling was one of "what can I contribute, how can I help?" and not "what can I get out of it?" People lived modestly and the leaders set an example with their modest life-styles. They were not like the bank managers of today, who, even as banks fail and the public has to pay the price, are not embarrassed to pocket salaries that run into the millions. There is constant talk today about the need for "infrastructures" but it is all talk. We may not have been familiar with the term, back then, and there was no Minister of Infrastructure then, but we managed to pave hundreds of kilometers of road out of nothing and we did this without foreign labor.

Work in those regions was fraught with danger. One of my friends, who worked on the Sodom-Eilat road, was killed by the Arab fedayyeen (as the terrorists of that time were called). They used to attack quiet Jewish settlements and kill people there. The Sinai Campaign put an end to these activities on their part.

We would go to work every morning at five and never returned before seven in the evening. We would take a thermos of tea and some sandwiches with us. It wasn't easy but I never heard anyone complain. Those were truly different times: nobody was rich – but people were happy.

I would often give the head of Solel Boneh, the late Mr. Tuviah, a ride home to Hod Hasharon. We would usually leave Beersheba at around 9 or 10 at night, because he worked very long hours, being devoted to his job. We would talk along the way and he once said to me: "You'll see, Beersheba will become the capital of the Negev and it will have a university." I looked at him and thought to myself – "what a dreamer! But he is apparently very determined and will probably reach any goal he sets for himself!" Several years later, Tuviah was elected mayor of Beersheba and under his management, the city grew and developed and his dream became a reality. Today, Beersheba has a good university that is very much in demand. Even my grandson, Ophir, is studying there now, studying bio-information and computer science.

The Accident

In April 1951, we were driving fast along a newly paved road leading south from Beersheva. Just before Kibbutz Shoval, an army truck, a GMC six-wheeler, came towards me, pulling an army command car at the end of a long cable. Just as we were about to pass one another, the cable suddenly snapped and the command car was thrown to the middle of the road and crashed into the front of my jeep, hard. The jeep I was driving rolled over several times and the three people riding with me were thrown out, suffering minor injuries. I remained trapped beneath the jeep, lying there wounded, seriously hurt. The head of the Beersheba police, Shmuel Bugler, one of my friends who had fought with me in Gush Etzion, arrived on the scene. He made sure that an ambulance came and took me to the Beersheba hospital. I had no idea what was going on because I was unconscious, suffering from a serious concussion. I suffered breaks in the pelvic area, my intestines were out of place from having been hit by the steering wheel when the car overturned, three fingers in my left hand were broken. In addition, I was hemorrhaging in the stomach area, and had open wounds in other areas of the body. In short – I was a mess. My whole body was a mass of wounds, fresh bruises and sore spots. When the doctors came to see

216 | THE POWER OF LIFE

me, they shook their heads, convinced that I didn't stand a chance. At first, they simply decided not to touch me or do anything, since they felt that it would all be to no avail. I was very lucky because many of the problems resolved themselves naturally and I was saved countless operations – who knows how those would have turned out?

After a few days, I suddenly regained consciousness. I was in great pain, hurting all over, and felt as if I was connected to all sorts of tubes. I didn't know what had happened and couldn't remember anything. I also had no idea where I was. I opened my eyes with a certain amount of trepidation and what was the first thing I saw? In the doorway were the heads of several pretty girls who had come to visit me, waving to me, smiling at me shyly. For just a moment I thought I was in a Moslem heaven, but the pains and a quick glance around me made it clear to me that I was lying in a hospital bed. I could only wave back weakly with my right hand, since my left hand was in a cast because of the three broken fingers. In spite of everything, I was pleased with myself. I had had no idea that I had so many admirers.

Despite the fact that I had only a vague recollection of the accident, I clearly understood that I had escaped death for the umpteenth time, and I felt reborn.

I slowly began to realize that I could not move my leg. I was afraid that I was paralyzed and would remain that way forever. I began wondering what was the use of living if that were to happen.

The doctors held a consultation next to my bed in the morning, and I heard them say, talking over my head, as if I wasn't there, that if my intestines hadn't "straightened themselves out" by t e next morning, they would have to operate on me and that it was a dangerous operation. The next mornii g, I felt something moving around in my belly. The doctors examined me and found that somehow, during the night, everything had returned in place and that the operation would not be necessary. Maybe that was just one more of my survival wonders.

The doctors decided to put me in a body cast that would cover me from my neck to the soles of my feet. When they had finished enveloping me in the plaster, I could barely move my head. I was told that I would have to stay in this body cast for six months. I fell into deep depression. I didn't see how I could stand it. I felt like a mummy or like someone who had been buried alive.

To my great joy, I had a guardian angel. Every few days, my girlfriend and future wife, Hava, would come from Tel Aviv to visit me. She had very strong instincts and a natural gift for understanding and diagnosing a situation, despite her youth and inexperience. She took care of me devotedly and fought to have me transferred to Beilinson hospital in Petach Tikva. She ran around from office to office for two weeks and finally managed to get all the necessary paperwork together. In order to save face, I was told that I would be moved to Beilinson hospital because there were specialists there who would be able to provide more comprehensive and professional care.

A special ambulance took me to Beilinson. There, I was greeted by a large man, Max, who looked like a thug. He grabbed me, lifted me up and placed me on a bed as if I was some sort of rag doll. However, when we got to know each other better during my stay at the hospital, I found that he was a good and warm person, and he helped me through the long difficult period when all I could do was lay in bed, unable to move.

After a few weeks, the doctors decided that they would remove the heavy cast and replace it with a lighter one, greatly easing my suffering and in general, making me feel better. I was in Professor Nathan's ward, a famous surgeon who was known to be very devoted to all of his patients.

When I think back on my condition at the time, I find it difficult to understand how I was able to stand it all – lying there motionless, without any air conditioning, in a large, hot room, without even a fan to stir the air. Days and nights were endless, interminable. I lay in a large ward that held 20 beds, all containing people suffering from various ills. In the bed next to mine was a young man with cancer. The treatments for cancer at the time were very strenuous, much more than treatments of today, and the young man suffered terribly. He died after a few months. When I heard that I was very sad, because we had been in the habit of speaking of many things and had developed a strong connection. Despite the fact that I was couldn't do anything, even for myself, I felt a certain amount of satisfaction that I had been able, even if only very little, raise his spirits during his last days. These conversations had done a lot for me too, because I was very lonely.

In another neighboring bed was an older man who had come from Germany. He had an unusual sense of humor and used to make us laugh with his stories and jokes. Some of my friends, of course, came to visit, but understandably, they couldn't devote many hours to me because of their jobs and other responsibilities. My most steady visitor was my girlfriend, Hava, whose optimism filled me with hope. This hope, miraculously, gave me the strength to fight. The doctors had already determined that I would never be able to walk again because I had not been operated upon immediately in the Beersheba hospital and the bones had not knit properly. I can't say that I wasn't angry with the medical team in Beersheba. I even had moments, some lonely moments, when I was tempted to put an end to it all.

Looking back on that period from the perspective of many years later, it is easy to write just a few lines about those six months I spent in a hospital bed. However, going through it was utter hell. Apparently, I had a very high tolerance for pain and suffering, because after everything that had happened to me during the Holocaust and afterwards, during the War of Independence in Gush Etzion, and in captivity, I was still tough. Needless to say, this accident had been a superfluous "addition" to my list of experiences.

I was able to draw some comfort from the small

songbook that had been among my belongings and which containing songs from the Palmach. I particularly liked the song called "Yesh Li Kinneret" ("I have a Kinneret" [the Sea of Galilee]), written by Zvi ben Yosef, who fell during the battle in Gush Etzion. The songbook also contained songs such as "Bab el Wad", "Hafinjan", and many more. I really liked to sing back then. The songs reminded me of good times in the past and so I sang a lot.

What bothered me the most was when a bug or a fly would get caught between the cast and my body. The humming noise and the horrible feel of the bug or fly were aggravating because I was totally helpless. It would drive me crazy. I could now understand Titus' reaction when a fly entered his ear. Even the nurses, as wonderful as they were, were unable to help me.

Five months passed, but to me, it seemed like five years. The doctors began saying that they would soon be taking the cast off. I remembered what the doctors had said when I had entered the hospital, that they doubted that I would ever be able to walk again. This troubled me greatly. I didn't talk about it to anyone, but I couldn't stop thinking about it. I thought that since I had survived so much danger and hardship, I had no choice but to overcome this too. I was wondering whether Hava would be willing to stay with me, should I remain a cripple for the rest of my life. I didn't dare bring up the subject with her.

The nurses had always spoiled me but at this point, I felt that they were giving me more love and attention than ever, maybe because of the possibility that I might be a cripple. Whatever the reason, their attention made me feel good. This was very important to me because I had nobody and I so missed the warmth of a family. Even so, no person, not even a friend can give a person the close feeling one gets from family, the empathy, the emotional caring. When one is in trouble – there is no substitute for family. I truly understood this many years later, when I went to the United States for the first time and discovered that in addition to my sister, I had a very large family there. I became very close with some of them. I will write about finding this extended family in a later chapter, where I describe how I found that I, too, had relatives.

The long-awaited day finally arrived. My cast was to be removed. I saw that all of the department's doctors and nurses had come. They brought me a walker and Dr. Nathan said to me: "Get up slowly and try to take a few steps", and I replied: "I am going to get up and walk!" All eyes were on me, or to be more exact, on my feet. You could have cut the tension in the room with a knife. I sat up on the bed, swung one, and then the other foot to the floor, stood up on the floor, waited a bit, gathered all my strength and took a first step, then another. Everyone applauded, encouraging me. From the corner of my eye, I saw a nurse begin to cry, and I was moved. This nurse had been very compassionate and had always given me special attention.

At the beginning, sitting up in bed and getting to my feet were the hardest things to do. Only my strong will, determination and unlimited patience that made it possible for me to overcome these obstacles. My first steps were slow and careful, but I got better as the days went by. I was a happy man the day that I was able to walk down the long corridor and reach the dining room. I knew that if I didn't help myself, no one would do it for me, and that spurred me on. The healing process was long and exhausting. I waited impatiently for the moment that I would be able to throw the crutches away and walk under my own power. Friends came to visit and cheered me up. When I felt more confident of myself, I discarded the crutches and began going out to sit in the garden with friends, to breathe some fresh air. Hava often came to the hospital and our relationship deepened.

Two weeks after I first got up from my bed, and after all the examinations were over and x-rays had been taken, I was released from the hospital and moved into a rest home in Bnei Brak for ten days of convalescence.

Once again, for God knows how many times, I had survived!

A New Beginning

As I began feeling better, my mind was filled with troubling thoughts: What will I do with myself? Where will I go? What will I do? One day, one of my friends, Moshe, who worked for the Ministry of Defense, came to see me with a jeep. I said to him: "Let me have the steering wheel, I want to drive a bit." "Have you gone crazy?" he replied. I begged him – I had to see if I still remembered how to drive, if I still could drive. I held the steering wheel with trembling hands and took the car for a spin. After a few minutes, I could see, to my great joy, that I had not forgotten how to drive and that I had not lost my nerve. I suddenly saw that how quickly one could forget one's troubles and discover new experiences. It is possible to exist without always dwelling on sad memories.

After having spent a few weeks recuperating, I went to the Solel Boneh offices. To tell the truth, the people there were not particularly pleasant to me. I wasn't part of the "old guard" and so they weren't especially friendly. I went there a few times and during one of my visits to the department in which I have been working before the accident to see if they had work for me, I ran into the late Moshe Taron, who had been in charge of the Solel Boneh warehouses in Beersheba and had since transferred to work for a pipe-manufacturing plant in Ashkelon, "Yuval Gad", which produced the large pipes used to build the National Water Carrier. At my request, he immediately arranged for me to work in that plant. I was given an interesting and responsible job. I was to record the production procedures and activities in all the departments, as well as the time it took to carry out each and every step of the process. Later, this record was later used as the basis for decision-making as to how and where the work could become more efficient. At the time, the plant workers came from all over – they were new immigrants from every country, a real "ingathering of the exiles." But they had found a common language and each and every one of them treated his/her work seriously.

To me, the most interesting department was the welding department. This was work that required the utmost precision. The welding machine was like a sewing machine – if used improperly, it could leave holes in a pipe, and even if they were small holes, the pipe would not be able to pass the pressure trials set at several atmospheres. In such cases, the pipe would leak and in time, rust would form, eating away at the metal. Before laying a pipe in the ground, we had to be absolutely certain that there were no leaks at all, that not even one drop of water could get through.

Welding courses were held at the plant and we found that immigrants from Yemen excelled in this profession, because they had the patience and ambition necessary to do a good job. I liked them because they were warmhearted and cheerful people, fired by a great desire to work well. They worked very hard and felt that they were contributing through their work, and were paid good salaries, based upon their production and output.

The plant itself was part of one of Ben Gurion's master plans – to bring water to the Negev and make it bloom. He was a determined visionary leader, and even today, he is still held up as an example for the generations to come. Over and over again, he preached the settling of the Negev and even set a personal example – when he decided that his home would be in Kibbutz Sde Boker, in the middle of the desert.

Settlements and towns began springing up in the Negev and everyone was able to find a job. People weren't choosy and everyone was happy to take any job offered, because work gave them a sense of pride, a sense of belonging and of self-value.

The water which was brought to the Negev from the Sea of Galilee turned at least part of it into a flowering garden and provided a living for thousands of families. Thus, dreams became a reality, because some determined and forward-looking people made it possible to take in and care for hundreds of thousands of new immigrants from all corners of the earth, bringing everybody "home".

I continued working for the Yuval Gad Company in Ashkelon, traveling there early every morning and returning to Tel Aviv every evening.

One day, my girlfriend Hava invited me to her home and introduced me to her parents and her grandparents.

Her grandfather was a very impressive person, sporting a small beard. He was a religious man and very educated. My first meeting with Hava's parents was very strange. I walked into their house without wearing a kippah (skullcap), something which didn't exactly please her father. He manufactured kitchen utensils, and before coming to Israel, had owned a company that manufactured kitchen utensils. He was a very religious person and would, of course, have preferred a religious student, or at least someone studying in a yeshiva, as a son-in-law. He certainly wanted someone who followed Jewish traditions and precepts. But Hava herself was not observant, far from it. In contrast, Hava's grandmother herself was a religious woman but realized that she was living in a modern world. I could see that she had once been a beautiful woman. In time, we developed a very close and honest relationship. She would even offer me a piece of the cake that would be kept in the locked glass cupboard. She would ceremoniously open the cupboardwith one of the keys hanging from her belt on an intricate pure silver key ring. She kept the keys and only she was allowed to use them. This was just one example of the way of life for "Viennese aristocrats", which was also expressed in the respect accorded to the expensive and beautiful Bidermeier furniture, with the many drawers and locked cabinets, scattered about the house.

Hava's mother and I also began developing a good relationship. With the passage of time, I took care of her, took care of anything she needed. I also helped her economically. When Hava and I had differences of opinion, her mother usually sided with me.

Going back to out first meeting – Hava's family began, of course, by asking personal questions: who was I, what did I do, where did I come from and where was my family? These were very difficult questions for me to answer. I told them a little about my family, that I had studied in a religious school, and that I had been in a religious kibbutz. These answers improved the atmosphere somewhat. During that first meeting, only the grandmother seemed to be a little disappointed: a Polish groom … not quite her cup of tea! They, the "Viennese" had always felt that they were superior to the "Poles". I told them that my mother had studied in Vienna, but did not mention her feelings about the condescending Viennese Jews.

I continued coming to their house. With time, the ice melted. I liked talking with Hava's grandfather. He was known for his generosity and was always willing to help any member of the family who needed help. The grandfather was a "man of the world" and before the war had owned several paper and cardboard factories in Austria. In 1923, he built the largest plant ever built in Hungary for paper and carton. This factory even had railroad tracks running up to the factory's warehouses. Hava and I saw this when we visited Hungary in 1991. We set up a meeting with the Manager of the factory. When we entered the fancy "lobby" of the offices, we saw that the photographs of the founders of the factory were still hanging. The manager presented us with a biography of the founder of the factory. This book also contained photographs of the members of the family. We were very moved. The plant manager told me that the value of the factory had been assessed at some 25 million U.S. dollars, without taking into account its real estate value. Unfortunately, the Hungarian government had legislated laws that did not permit heirs from taking possession of property that might have been left to them in Hungary.

I told Hava's family about my sister in the United States and the fact that there was probably quite a large family there, because some members of the family had left Buczacz, emigrating to the United Stated, but that I did not know any of them. Maybe, unintentionally, I might have alluded to my loneliness and my need for a supportive and loving family.

I slowly began getting to know Hava's family and to appreciate their finer qualities. Thus, family affairs were generally happy occasions and the family would often break into Viennese and Hungarian songs.

After a year of "keeping company", we began talking about marriage. Hava said that I would have to discuss the "subject" with her parents. The truth was that I had no idea where to begin or how we would manage. I had no financial resources, but I had plenty of work. I was only 23 then and had barely enough money to buy my fiancee a small diamond engagement ring. But when I did buy it, Hava was very happy.

During one of our conversations, Hava's father said that he wanted me to go with him and have a talk with the "visionary" rabbi (it was thought that he could see in the future). Apparently, Hava's father was not completely comfortable with the thought that his daughter was marrying a man who wasn't a religious person, who had no family and so it wasn't possible to get first-hand information about him. He wanted the opinion of a respected Torah scholar, a respected member of the community. I, of course, agreed – what won't a person do when he wants to get married?

The next day, we went to Bnei Berak, to meet the "visionary". I entered his home, filled with awe. His reputation had transcended the boundaries of the religious community. He was known for his wisdom, his honesty, his modesty and his pleasant demeanor. I sat with him for over an hour and we developed a bond. I told him about my life in a nutshell. He had many questions for me: about my family, about the war, about captivity. I mentioned my wonderful teacher, told him that my mother and father had been orthodox Jews, as well as my grandfather, who had obeyed the precepts of Jewish law, and who had been a very respected member of the Buczacz Jewish community. Unfortunately, none of my immediate family had survived, with the exception of myself and my sister, who was living in the United States. I didn't even have one photograph of my family.

We had a pleasant conversation, during which I was "coached" on the responsibility that I was taking upon myself by getting married. I left this meeting feeling calm, certain of the good impression I had made. I had enjoyed my time spent with the rabbi. The rabbi then spoke with Hava's father and thus, I successfully passed another one of life's trials.

A few days later, we set a date for the engagement and I met her entire family. Hava had many relatives, most of them "Austro-Hungarians" who knew how to enjoy themselves. Only a few of the guests were from my side, all of them distant relatives. It was a very nice evening. I met many members of Hava's family and formed friendships with some of them that have lasted through the years. Since I had grown up alone for so many years, I was very sentimental when it came to family ties and was very glad to become part of such a large warm family.

The wedding day was set for May 13, 1952. I liked the 13th as a date, because I had been born on August 13th .

The wedding preparations got underway immediately. Hava sewed herself a wedding dress from a pattern and for the first time in my life, I bought myself a black suit, a tie and a top hat. I felt strange, because I as a "kibbutznik", I only owned khaki shorts for wearing during the week and khaki pants for Shabbat, but I decided to respect the occasion and dress according to the rules of the game.

Some of Hava's Viennese relatives came to the wedding. They were very elegant and beautifully dressed. Hava's grandfather's brother, his wife and some cousins came from Germany. Even the Austrian ambassador and his entourage attended the wedding.

The wedding was held in the Great Synagogue of Tel Aviv, on Allenby Street. Rationing was in force in those days, but one of the relatives, an expert caterer, prepared and served delicious beautiful refreshments. It was a very "respectful", bourgeois affair and for the first time in my life, I felt that I was an "important" person. The grandfather's brother came in a tuxedo and his wife wore an elegant muslin dress, unusual for Tel Aviv of that period. The guests all had a good time and celebrated, dancing and singing German and Hungarian songs.

Our wedding in the Great Synagogue on Allenby Road, 13 May 1952

After the wedding, Hava and I went to a small hotel on Rothschild Boulevard, where we had our "wedding night". The next day, we were off to Tiberias for our honeymoon.

After a while, members of Hava's family went back

to Vienna and were able to recover their factories. We bought an apartment in Giv'at Rambam, in Givatayim. I took out a mortgage, despite the fact that my work situation was quite uncertain. In the meantime, until our apartment was ready, we lived in her grandfather's apartment for a few months. The apartment was full of beautiful, expensive, antique furniture ("Biedermeier"). I felt as if I was living in a museum and was afraid to touch anything.

During that same period, I decided to look for a different job, something closer to Tel Aviv, and I found a job in factory that produced grape juice. This was a small plant and within a month, I had doubled their production. The owner, who was a real "yekke" (name given to immigrants from Germany who had Germanic manners concerning dress and work ethics), praised my industriousness, but did not raise my salary. I worked there for several months but could not see any future there for me.

Suddenly I had an idea: when I had been working for "Yuval Gad" in Ashkelon, I had noticed that once in a while someone would come to the plant from Tel Aviv to buy the metal scraps left over from the manufacture of the pipes. If this was profitable for him, maybe it could be for me as well? I began wandering around various metal warehouses and found the one belonging to the man who bought scrap metal from "Yuval Gad", acting as if he had more or less cornered the market. I went to one of his competitors and offered my "merchandise" – which I didn't have yet. In the meantime, I tried to find out information about prices and what this material could be used for. I met sales manager in Ashkelon, asked about buying metal scraps and was given the "purchase price". I took a sample back with me to Tel Aviv and met with the merchant with whom I had already begun negotiations. We agreed on a price that suited us both. It was certainly possible to make a profit. So I found myself well on the way to becoming a metal merchant, a profession that was diametrically opposed to all of my previous beliefs and outlook. In "Mikveh Yisrael", I had been educated to work the land and to be part of the land. This was the ideal which had been the basis of our education. This is why we had wanted to come to Israel for two thousand years. A "merchant", on the other hand, was the epitome of the Diaspora Jew, not to be respected, even scorned. However, when one takes on the responsibility of a family, one will do anything and everything one can, even if it means going into business.

Even as a child in Buczacz, during the war, I had been a "merchant". Conditions were completely different now, but I still had the instincts of a merchant and my previous experience was invaluable.

I rented a large dump truck (at the time metal warehouses had no cranes to load and unload the merchandise). I loaded the scrap metal onto the truck, drove to Tel Aviv and reached the merchant's warehouse. When I showed him the document with the weight of the load, he sent me to the scales in Nahalat Yitzhak, in order to weigh the truck, loaded and empty.

I wasn't insulted by his lack of trust – I fully understood his point of view and did as he asked. After the weighing, I returned to the warehouse and he showed me where to unload the merchandise. We raised the back of the truck and the driver began advancing slowly, dropping the metal on the floor, in the same order in which it had been arranged on the truck. It was then that I received my "first lesson" in doing business in Israel: the merchant looked at me and said that it was not "the same" as the sample I had shown him. I was in shock. How could that be? Still not understanding his motives, I took a piece, measured it, and showed him that it was the exact size as the sample. But the merchant insisted. All I could think of at that point was – what am I going to do now? There was nowhere else for me to take the merchandise, and besides, it was too difficult for me to reload it manually, all by myself. I finally understood what he was doing – he simply wanted to lower the price. In the end, we compromised and I still made a decent profit. This was my first business venture and when it was over, I went to my wife and said: "I made money in business."

The lesson I learned from this incident was that in order to increase my profit margin, I had to go directly to the end user. This unfortunate incident had taught me a lot.

I began checking out smithies, looking for someone who could use the metal scraps. Finally, one day, I "fell" upon a factory that needed just that type of merchandise: the owner made metal cages for transporting poultry from kibbutzim and moshavim to "Tnuva" in Tel Aviv. He was willing to take all the metal I could provide and we agreed upon a price. Then there was another problem: he was only willing to pay me with post-dated checks. This meant that he would deposit checks or bonds from clients and on the basis of these securities, he would get credit from the bank. What was I to do? I remembered the late Aharon Meir, then Managing Director of Bank HaMizrachi, who had been a friend of mine since the establishment of Massuot Yitzhak. I went to talk to him and he agreed to give me credit, using the post-dated checks I received as security. He smoothed the way for me and thus made it possible for me to run my business. I was ecstatic. I was on my way to being a real merchant.

In time, I realized that it wasn't possible to conduct business that way, living from hand to mouth, because there were always different sizes metal scraps, and what was right for one person wasn't suitable for another. I looked for and found a warehouse to rent in the industrial zone of Holon. I began unloading the merchandise there. I hired workers and sorted the merchandise according to size, width, length, thickness and quality, thereby increasing my profits. I also spread the risk, because in the meantime, my clientele had grown. I was industrious, very ambitious and prepared to work hard in order to become a serious merchant. In time, I became well-versed in all aspects of this field and spread out into other domains of metal commerce.

I had no one to teach or guide me – experience was my only teacher. Sometimes I paid a high price for these lessons, but that was all part of life and reality.

When the copper plant was opened in Timna, I contacted them and became their scrap iron supplier. In order to produce a ton of copper, they needed 1,250 kilos of a certain kind of scrap metal. I organized a gang of workers (mostly Yemenites) from Sha'araim, which was next to Petach Tikva, and they helped me collect and load the merchandise. The Timna plant manager was so satisfied with our work that I received letters of appreciation and thanks from the managing director of the plant, the late Benny Yehuda. No competitor was able to match my degree of efficiency and that of my workers. I was one of the first to purchase special loading equipment – a hydraulic crane and shovel, both of which made my life and that of my suppliers much easier.

I continued working hard like this for many years, working outside every day, summer and winter. The production of the Timna plant was very dependent on the material that I was able to supply, because it was used in the chemical process that separated dirt from the copper.

The excavations that took place there uncovered ancient furnaces that dated back to the days of King Solomon – what was known as "King Solomon's Mines". This was undeniable proof that copper was being produced in the region back in those days and that the Jews had inhabited the region as far back as

King Solomon's time.

As long as world copper prices were high, everything went smoothly. However, this couldn't last forever. The Korean and the Vietnam wars ended and demand for copper decreased steadily. Suddenly, copper prices plunged and the plant found itself facing financial difficulties. One day, out of the clear blue sky, it was decided that the Timna operation would be closed down.

Once again, I found myself at a crossroads in my life, unsure as to which way to turn.

I had an idea that concerned working with raw materials intended for the metal industry. I had acquired quite a lot of experience in the field and was familiar with many manufacturing plants producing a variety of products. I knew which ones needed what. I had also developed many good personal contracts with owners of factories and plants, which would allow me to break into this field that much more easily. In time, I acquired metal cutting and bending equipment and went from being a supplier of cut raw material to a producer of metal.

In 1999, I began looking for ways to gracefully stop running the business. I did not have someone who could step into my shoes. After searching for quite some time, I found a young company that in the same field, and transferred my whole business, equipment included, to them.

And so I retired, after having worked very, very hard

for 35 years.

Today, I spend my time volunteering to work with a variety of associations whose main concern is working with and for people in need.

And, as can be seen by this manuscript, I finally have time to write.

My Family

A few weeks after returning from captivity in Jordan, an American army officer on vacation in Israel visited me. He introduced himself as a friend of my family in New York and gave me the addresses of all of the members of my family there. He told me that I had a very large family in the United States and that they were very nice. He, of course, gave me my sister's address, with whom I had not been in contact for several years. Excited and very moved, I immediately wrote to her, and from that moment on, received a letter from her every few weeks. We exchanged letters on a regular basis. She would write in Polish – a language I hated – and I would write in German – also a language which I did not particularly like, but it was a language in which made I could better express myself.

In her first letters, my sister expressed her concern that I was "alone in the world" and she wondered "how I was managing." I reassured her and explained that I was a big boy now and was getting along – there was no need for her to worry.

She had not had a particularly easy life. After arriving in the United States with her husband, Ephraim Koenigsberg, he started a plant that manufactured curtains, but he passed away 3-4 years later and my sister was left a widow with a son of four. She raised him alone for several years and had to work hard in order to survive. Later on, she remarried, to a man named Yehoshua First, with whom she had her second son.

In my letters, I told Sali about what had happened to me. I told her about the relationship that was developing between Hava and myself and then was able to tell her the good news –we were going to get married. She was very sorry that she would be unable to come to the wedding. At that time, it was a very complicated and expensive proposition to come all the way form the United States to Israel.

It was only after we were married that Hava and I truly came to know one another. We had moments of joy, moments of sadness, but always provided support for each other, because that was the only way that we were able to overcome all of the obstacles that were put in our way. At the beginning of our life as a married couple, we encountered difficult times, as did all young couples in Israel at the time. We lived under the shadow of wars, during which I would have to go for army reserve duty for several months, something which was very difficult for me. This caused no end of difficulties in the business, which of course influenced what went on at home, and there were, of course, also all of the normal frictions which husband and wife go through. However, so far, we have managed to overcome all obstacles.

My daughter, Amalia, was born on January 21, 1954. My late son, Ronny, was born on June 19, 1961. We raised them with love and were very proud of them, and tried to give them as many opportunities as we could, within our means. They had very different personalities, as is normal among children – each child is a world unto him/herself.

Amalia studied in one of the Government Religious schools and when she began studying in the secular "Herzliya Gymnasia", a high school in Tel Aviv, her homeroom teacher called Hava and asked where our daughter had gone for elementary school, because she was different than the other children – her behavior was exemplary. Hava received many compliments regarding Amalia, which made us very proud and happy.

Ronny was a good student and very popular with his friends. However, if the subject was of no interest to him, he didn't make any effort, as is common among students.

In 1968, one year after the Six Days' War, we traveled to the United States for the first time, to celebrate the bar mitzva of my sister's eldest son, David. My sister Sali and I had not seen each other for 23 years. If I were to say that our encounter, after such a long separation, was fraught with emotions, this would not be strong enough to explain the force of the feelings that we experienced.

We stayed at my sister's house. We sat together for hours, for days, reminiscing. I said to her: "We have said goodbye so many times, and fate has always brought us together again."

My sister tried to spoil me, preparing all sorts of delicacies which I had loved as a child.

This visit was an opportunity to discover the rest of my family. On Shabbat, we went to the synagogue and there, for the first time, I met my late uncle, Max, and my aunt May, their daughter Moira, their son, Arthur, his wife, Carol and their children, Debbie and Lisa, as well as other members of the family. This was, for me, a very significant meeting. I was suddenly faced with members of a large family, people with whom I had never had any contact.

That morning, there was a procession of acquaintances and relatives from Buczacz who had survived the war and who remembered me as a child. They all wanted to know where I had been during the War of Independence and how I had managed to survive that war too. I told them about the battles in Gush Etzion and about my period of captivity in Jordan. They listened attentively and drank in each word thirstily, because this was the first time that they had heard, firsthand, how we, so few, had managed to overcome the odds of fighting so many enemies. I refused to talk about my experiences during the Holocaust.

My stories moved them very much. I hoped that they would make these people decide to come to Israel, even if it was only for a visit.

And that is exactly what happened. When my aunt turned 80, her son, Arthur, took the whole family to Israel to celebrate the occasion. We invited the whole group, all 20 of them, to our house for a festive meal.

Other relatives also came to Israel, especially my cousin Irving, who would volunteer to work in a different kibbutz each year.

I may not have managed to encourage anyone to immigrate to Israel, but I certainly contributed significantly to tourism!

Several years later, we also went to the United States for the bar mitzva of my sister's youngest son, Sammy, as well as for the weddings of both of her sons, and much later, for the bar mitzvas of their children. It was very important for us to be together and to take part in every celebration, particularly since so few members of the family were left, in contrast with the widespread family that had lived in Galicia before the Second World War.

Family celebration in the U.S. for the bar mitzva

of my sister's grandson.

Sometimes, during my visits to the U.S., I would remember my first meeting with my then future wife's parents. At that time, they had asked me about my family and I had not been able to tell them much. Now, I suddenly found myself a part of a large family, a warm, joyous family.

Many years later, I attended a family get-together organized by my cousin Arthur. A total of 150 family members attended. We became very close to Arthur and his family, as well as his mother, May, who was a very special woman. She was highly intelligent and knew how to keep the family together. Max, my late uncle, told me stories about his family that I had never heard before. We also went to visit my other uncle and my aunt. Today, most of my first cousins are lawyers and doctors. A fourth Anderman generation is now growing up there, all over the United States.

I am happy that we also have close relationships with my sister's children. As I always say, over and over again, there is no substitute for family.

My daughter enlisted in the IDF in 1972 and served in a very important unit (Refael). During her basic training, I was in the nearby Sarafen army camp for a few weeks, taking a course for biological warfare officers, so it was easy for me to attend her graduation from basic training. The next day, I returned to work and my daughter went to join her unit. The general feeling in the country was one of contentment and prosperity. It was the beginning of the great wave of immigration from the U.S.S.R., construction was on the rise and the general economic situation in the country was improving, and we were enjoying a peaceful time out with our neighbors.

Approximately one year later, the Yom Kippur War broke out, when the armies of Syria and Egypt suddenly attacked us simultaneously on both fronts. We managed to barely avoid destruction by the skin of our teeth. We suffered many casualties and it was one of the worst periods the country had known since the War of Independence. My son, Ronny, was preparing for his bar mitzva at the time. A few months after the war, we reserved a hall for the bar mitzva celebration as planned. As this important day drew near, I suggested that he forgo having music in view of the generally depressed atmosphere in the country.

I shall never forget his reply to me: "There will always be wars here, but I will only have one bar mitzva in my life." His words made a great impression on me and there was music at his bar mitzva party. His joy is etched in my memory and I can't forget how happy he was during the celebration.

In honor of the bar mitzvah, my wife's and my family came from abroad and on Thursday, we all went up to Jerusalem, to the Wailing Wall, to pray and to put on t'filin. We performed the Torah reading feeling very emotional. Hava's mother, who was very religious, was very moved by the occasion because Ronny was a Cohen, making the occasion even more moving and cherished. We had brought a cold box full of goodies with us and were able to give our guests something to eat. We took many pictures in memory of the occasion. Each of the guests placed a note in cracks between the stones of the Wall containing some request or other.

*My son, **Ronny**, at his bar mitzva*

Afterwards, we toured Jerusalem and reached the Promenade in "Armon Ha-Natziv", where we could look upon Jerusalem in all of its splendor: The Old City, which is pure history, and the new part of the city, which was expanding rapidly. This is the most beautiful view in the world. The whole history of the Jewish people lies in the Judean Hills, on the way to the walls of the Old City.

Putting on tfilin at the Kotel, the Wailing Wall,
during the bar mitzva, November 1973

My late sister and her son became very emotional. This was my sister's first visit to Israel and every moment brought more wonder and amazement.

My daughter Amalia was wed a year later and brought my son-in-law, Shmuel, into the family. He is a model father and very devoted to his family and we are very proud of him. Two years later, my daughter gave birth to their son, Ophir, and they decided to go to the United States so that he could continue his studies. Yael was born there. When the children were ready to start school, the family returned to Israel so that they could be raised and educated in Israel.

Our son, Ronny, grew up to be very handsome, strong and full of life. He was very conscious of his looks and dressed in very good taste. He served in the Air Force and after completing his compulsory army service wanted to travel abroad, like all his peers.

*My daughter **Amalia's** wedding, 18 March 1975*

On September 5, 1985, we were informed that our beloved son, Ronny, had lost his life in a traffic accident in Germany, where he was visiting some of my wife's relatives.

This was a terrible blow. We were left with only memories of our beautiful son.

Despite the fact that we had many friends who tried to help us cope with this terrible tragedy, the loss of a beloved son, we knew that nothing could take the place of family. Only family could provide that feeling of closeness. It is only with family that one can be completely open and ask for advice in time of need. It is only with family that you allow yourself to express your pain and sorrow, to mourn completely.

Losing a son is difficult. It is a terrible thing. This pain remains with you always. It was particularly sharp during the first years, when we went to weddings of children of friends of ours. On such occasions, one must smile and be nice. The face smiles but the heart always weeps. However, the life force is strong and life must go on, and so one pretends and "plays the game".

After Ronny's death, I began suffering from nightmares. He would appear in my dreams. We would be playing or traveling together. I still have these dreams to this day.

My sister Sali was a warm, modest woman, always ready to help her fellow-man and this made everyone love her. In April 2000, she suddenly fell ill with an incurable illness. At the beginning, her letters did not give any indication of the seriousness of her situation – this only became clear when they informed me that she had been hospitalized. I decided to fly to the United States to be at her side in her time of need.

I arrived in New York, took a hotel room near the hospital, and would go to the hospital every day, at 07:00 a.m. to feed her in bed, and I would stay there until 8:00 p.m. My sister had contracted leukemia, cancer of the blood. Since the cancer had only been detected in its advanced stage, her chances were very slim. I talked with the head of the department to see if something could, nevertheless, be done for her and she told me that a new drug was to be distributed in another month, and my sister was to be one of its first recipients. In the meantime, my sister was in great pain and there was nothing to be done, only give her painkillers. Whenever she was awake, we would talk, dwelling, of course, on what had happened during the war and how we had survived. In the past, I had not wanted to talk to her about those years because it was too disturbing for me. Whenever we met, I would always say: "Let's talk about something else, let's look ahead, not back. We both have children and want them to be happy, and it's best that they know as little as possible about that horrible and terrible period." I was not anxious to share my past with others. Not when it concerned that period of my life. But Sali had been through a lot of it with me. She remembered, better than me, the names of the farmers who had helped us and where we had hidden, because I had been a little boy when the war broke out.

We had a lot of time to talk. Each of us spoke about our families. I complimented her on the fact that she had raised two wonderful sons – one a doctor and the other an accountant. This would bring a satisfied smile to her lips, because she had worked hard to be able to provide them with an education. Sometimes, other members of the family would come to see her – she was especially happy when the grandchildren came. They loved her so much and the feeling was mutual.

During one of my visits to the hospital, her sons and I decided to take a private nurse to stay with Sali after I would leave in the evening. In this way, we were able to make it easier for her – she no longer had to wait for hours until a nurse could come and give her medication or do something else for her at night. During those eight days that I sat at her bedside I realized that my intuition had been correct, that I had to be with her during these difficult times. I felt that this was good for the both of us, because we talked about many things, things that we had not been able to talk about for 50 years.

The day that I had to leave, we knew that the parting was forever. We looked at each other, wordlessly. No words were necessary.

My sister passed away two weeks later. I still miss her.

Our family is very close. Amalia, our daughter, and Shmuel, our son-in-law are very industrious and work very hard, trying to give their children, our grandchildren as much as possible. Our grandchildren have already finished their army service and have begun studying at the university. Ophir is studying in Beersheba, and Yael, in Jerusalem. Our grandchildren are a source of joy and light up our lives. We love them very much and they reciprocate that love. My dear wife, Hava knows how to bring the family together and does that very well, providing the emotional force for us all to continue. Our relationship is stronger and more beautiful than ever.

Unfortunately, we still have not achieved that peace and rest which we hoped would arrive during our lifetime. The battle for our existence still continues and our enemies still have not come to terms with the fact that we have the right to exist here. We are always anxious and worried regarding the future of our children and grandchildren. However, I am certain, that if the whole nation remains determined and stands firm, we shall overcome these obstacles. I never stop hoping that very soon, we shall enjoy the fruits of peace.

Epilogue

After the decision to put my life's story on paper had been taken, I sat down and began writing, quickly, frenetically, as if in the grip of a frenzy. I sent my first attempt, which only consisted of a few pages, to "Yad Va-Shem" and was told that it was too brief and that I should expand the story.

It was difficult, because to begin digging through horrible memories is a difficult thing to do. One has to relive all of the horrors. You wonder – what shall I write about? How can I put it down on paper? I had so many ideas running around in my head, confused and tangled, and I thought that it would be impossible for me to make sense of them and express them in a clear and orderly manner. It might even be enough if I just point out that before the war, there had been over 20,000 Jews in Buczacz and the surrounding farms, and at the end of the war, only a few dozen remained. This fact, these dry numbers, speak for themselves. So should I talk about what happened to us, the survivors? What we saw, what we felt, our sufferings?

Who can truly understand us? No one will ever be truly able to understand what happened.

Nevertheless, I decided that I would write.

I would write even if there were emotions and events that I could not bring myself to touch upon because the nerve ends are still raw, exposed, the wounds are still festering and the pain, unrelieved.

Nevertheless, I decided that I would write.

I would write even if the readers, wherever and whoever they may be – in Israel or in any other country – cannot even begin to grasp the extent of my painful memories, I hope that they will be able to understand just a little, a tiny bit, of what I went through.

I wrote my book in the hope that the young people who are preparing to go into the army will read it and will have no doubts as to why they are fighting; so that they will know what it meant to be a Jew in the Diaspora and they will understand that without this country, there is no place in the world for a Jew to exist.

I have called my book "The Power of Life", subtitled, "Being a Human Being" because, in fact, this is a summary of my life. Even after the war, I had to struggle with fate, recover from blows dealt to me by life, and I was only able to do that because of "the power of life" and the fact that I was a human being.

Now that I have grown older, I look back at myself and at my life, and I feel a great sense of satisfaction in the fact that I, who as a youth was one of the only survivors from my family and the Jews of Buczacz, managed to raise a family in Israel, see my children and my grandchildren grow up and develop, and was able to take part in the war that led to the establishment of my country. I also had the pleasure of seeing the remnants of the Jewish people come together from all corners of the world and build new lives in our independent country.

When I was wandering alone and sick in the snow, in the fields and in the barns, hunted like a wild animal, I did not think, and I certainly did not dare hope, that one day, I would be granted the privilege of seeing this great miracle with my own eyes.

I regret that my mother and most of my large family, and the warm Jewish community of Buczacz did not have this chance. May their memory be blessed forever.

This is my story. It is not long. It is not embellished. I only related, in sequence, the difficult times I experienced and how I spent my childhood – everything that is etched in my memory and in my soul. I have also described what happened to me later, in Israel.

I thank God that I have also had the good fortune of some happy moments.

ADDENDUM

THE PEOPLES' DESIRE FOR PEACE

For many years, I have had commercial ties with Arabs from various areas, ranging from the Gaza Strip to the West Bank. Our relations have always been cordial, at times even friendly, and were based on mutual trust. I was in contact with them on a daily basis. Often, I would meet Arabs in my office and would, at times, even go to them. For example, I would go to Nablus, have lunch in the main marketplace, the only Jew in the place, the restaurant filled with Arabs. I was never harassed. It was the same when I went to Gaza or Hebron. A customer would call me and say – "come over and eat some fish with me at the beach, in Gaza." I never hesitated and was never afraid. They always introduced me to their friends, saying that I was a good person, a true friend, that I helped them, and that they had learned a lot from me in the use of metal in industry and in the trade. When they wanted to buy a piece of equipment, they would consult me. I was always ready to help them and would often give them the address of a place where they could find what they wanted.

Sometimes, understandably, politics would become the main topic of conversation. I would say to them:

"Look, Egypt governed the Gaza Strip for many years, and what did the Egyptians do for you? They wouldn't even let you enter Egypt. They didn't provide you with employment, or ensure that your children be educated! Look at what we have given you: you have learned the technologies of agriculture, metalwork, medicine, etc. from us. All of this was done willingly so that we could live peacefully side by side. Take a look at the West Bank. During the time that Jordan governed the West Bank, no factories were built, your people farmed as did your ancestors a thousand years ago, no hospitals were constructed – there weren't even the minimal social conditions."

One of them got up and said: "No one is better than the Jews", and then I said: "now we agree on something!" and they nodded their heads in agreement.

I had an Arab friend from Gaza who invited me to take part in his son's wedding. This was just when the President of Egypt, Anwar Sadat, came to Jerusalem and informed the Israel Knesset that he wanted peace. This was the beginning of a new era, one of hope. When I met the groom's father in 1968, I had a small smithy under his house, which measured a total of about 40 square meters. By the time the wedding took place in 1979, the house had grown to be multi-storied, measuring about 2,000 sq. meters, and from the roof, one could gaze over the whole of Gaza.

There were some 500 Arabs at the wedding, and one Jew – myself. I knew some of the other guests at the table from previous visits. The tables were filled with good food, particularly a lot of lamb. I enjoyed the feast. I ate with my hands, as did the others, and enjoyed the joyous atmosphere, the debka dancing, and in general, being part of the celebration.

One of the guests at the table asked me: "What do you think will happen to us, the Palestinians, after Sadat gets the Sinai back and there'll be peace with Egypt?" I said to them: "If you had a wise and responsible leader, who truly wanted peace and improve the lot of his people, he should have come to Jerusalem with Sadat and it would have been possible to solve the Palestinian problem and to reach an agreement!"

Everyone agreed with me. At the time, there weren't so many settlements and extremists on both sides were pretty much peripheral. Yes, they all agreed with me.

I said to them: "Egypt ruled you for 19 years. What did the Egyptians do for you and what have we done for you. They wouldn't even let you travel to Egypt. If someone was ill and wanted to reach the hospital, he had to have a special permit and by the time the permit came, that person was probably dead. Today, you can come into Israel, work, do business freely and those of you who work in Israel enjoy social rights and conditions, while during the Egyptian period, you couldn't even dream of this. Look at our hosts here. He built a huge house, he has a large plant with the latest equipment. You don't pay taxes and we provide you with everything, including medical help and modern hospitals in Israel.

"You know that on the West Bank, before the Six Days' War, there was no industry. There was only one small factory in Nablus that produced olive oil, and even that belonged to the Jordanian royal family."

The people at the table listened to me very carefully, and I concluded by saying: "We are even willing to help you build a country and to provide any help necessary."

I said all of this in their language, in Arabic.

I felt that I had convinced them, and added: "Here we are, you and me – we're not at war. There's peace between us. I come to you, you come to me, and we've developed a friendship. The problem always lies with our leaders. We've seen this throughout history – leaders were always the one who led the people to war, just as Nasser and other Arab leaders have done. Take a look at President Sadat, a brave man, respected for his bravery. He came to the conclusion that his people had had enough of war and decided to go another direction. Explain that to Abu 'Amar (Arafat). Tell him to take his military uniform off, to shave and to stop dealing in terror and war, because war has never achieved anything."

At the end of the evening, I parted from my hosts and returned to my home in Tel Aviv. I felt that they had understood the message and maybe what I had said would trickle down to others.

I must point out that at a later time, these same Arabs reminded me of my words and said that I had been right.

We Israelis have fought many battles with the Arab countries, even defeated them, but the long awaited peace did not arrive. Suddenly, in 1973, Sadat led his people and allies in the Yom Kippur War, and when he was finally convinced that he would not achieve anything through war, he came to Jerusalem and standing at the Knesset podium, declared that there would be no more wars and no more bloodshed. He led his people to peace, but unfortunately, later paid for this peace with his life.

Approximately one year after the signing of the peace agreement with Egypt, a group of 16 of us set out on a tour of Egypt. We were treated to coffee everywhere we went. We did not feel any hatred directed at us, with the exception of a group of intellectuals in Cairo – this group was an extremist group and has remained so until today.

Sadat took full advantage of the agreement in order to improve his people situation. Israel provided Egypt with technological and agricultural know-how. Many agricultural farms were established and Israeli instructors went to Egypt to teach the farmers new and advanced agricultural methods.

Some years later, King Hussein of Jordan and the late Yitzhak Rabin, then Prime Minister of Israel, signed a peace agreement between Jordan and Israel. The King's speech at the ceremony touched everybody – they were words that came from the heart, words that allowed us to hope that we would be able to reach an agreement with the Palestinians as well. At the same time, Rabin and Arafat signed the "Oslo Accords" and this was the beginning of negotiations between Israel and the Palestinians. Everyone hoped that we were on the brink of a new era and that both nations might find the peace that they so hoped for.

Unfortunately, when this came to a real test, it became evident that Arafat had never truly meant any of the things he said. It had all been an act. Lies. He has led his people into a war of uncompromising terror. He does not care about his people or the fact that their lives are full of suffering and hardship. Arafat has not honored any of the agreements signed with him and as a result, innocent Israelis are the victims of Palestinian terrorist acts. The resultant disappointment and mistrust created a tendency in the Israeli public to lean towards the right. Extremism has stained both sides and has become very worrying. The second Intifada broke out. We know how wars begin, but no one ever knows how they will end.

Extremism is a destructive element and can lead to more serious situations. Most of the Israeli public loves life and considers life to be more precious than land. The majority of the people do not worship ancient symbols dating back two thousand years. However, we are being sucked into a vicious circle of hatred between the two nations. This vicious circle must be broken.

We must now act to attain peace between us and the Palestinians, between us and the Arab countries, and this should happen sooner than later.

My Rabbi

It is said that every Jews has his or her own rabbi. Mine was Rabin – the symbol of a warrior and leader who dedicated his life to his country.

That same fateful Saturday night, I was in the square, showing my support of Rabin's policies. When they sang "Shir Ha-Shalom" (The Song of Peace), I began walking towards my house. As I was going up the stairs, I heard the sirens of ambulances. I opened the door and then my wife screamed: "They've murdered Rabin."

I sat down, shocked. I couldn't talk. My world had just crashed around me. The newscaster announced that the bullet that had hit Rabin had been a dumdum bullet. I froze. A thought ran through my head. The Ukrainians had almost killed me too with a dumdum bullet.

I have asked myself a thousand times how a Jew, especially a religious Jew, can do such a horrible thing. But there were many who were party to Rabin's death. Some of them were the rabbis who preach hatred, members of the Knesset who fan the flames of hatred from the pulpits and the podiums. Their god is not my god. This worship of false symbols, superstitions, "idol worshipping" – this is not the people of Israel. These are weeds that we must uproot from among us if we wish to live, to survive, because they are the real danger that could bring about the destruction of the Third Temple.

Rabin's way is our tradition and most of the people believe in it and hope that it will one day become a reality.

*Yom Ha'Atzmaut (Day of Independence) in 1992, with the late **Yitzhak Rabin**, at the house of my friend, Haim Peled*

Appreciation from a "brother in arms"

Pessach joined Kibbutz Massuc Yitzhak in Gush Etzion along with a group of new im nigrant youths who had completed their training in t e Mikveh Yisrael Agricultural School and thus became one of the youngest members of the kibbutz.

When the war broke out and battles raged in Gush Etzion and the Hebron-Bethlehem-Jerusalem road in 1948, Pessach joined the kibbutz combat unit, under my command.

Dawn on Wednesday, 12 May 1948 saw the beginning of the last battle. The unit took up positions on "Rock Hill" and repulsed the Arab Legion's soldiers who were fighting under the command of British army officers. With the fall of darkness, my unit was given the task of evacuating the hospital in Kfar Etzion, moving the people to Kibbutz Massuot Yitzhak. I told Pessach to carry out the assignment, with a scout leading the wounded. There were a number of severely injured persons among the wounded, who had to be transferred on stretches (among them, Avrasha Tamir, who later became a general in the IDF).

This rapid and courageous operation saved the lives of all the wounded. A few hours later, the gangs burst into Kfar Etzion and all our combatants were killed in face-to-face combat.

Pessach carried out his assignment without hesitation, and showed bravery that could only arouse admiration. I felt that he was filled with the spirit that had guided him throughout the hard times he underwent during WWII.

Zeev Yehudai

MINISTER OF DEFENSE
08.08.2011

Dear Mr. Anderman,

Dear Pesach

Your story is the authentic testimony of a person who survived the misery of the Holocaust and who, in its aftermath, immigrated to Israel to continue fighting for the nascent country, together with your companions, survivors of the Holocaust, the last remnants of their families. The story of your life is interwoven in the history of the Jewish people during the last generation, imparting values of decisiveness, self-sacrifice, devotion and love for the country.

We must educate the future generations about the heritage of Pesach and his friends, for they are an inspiration for the future soldiers in the IDF.

Shalom

Ehud Barak
Minister of Defense

EPILOGUE

I am so proud of my mother Sali and my uncle Pesach. Their passion for life and their survival instincts are directly responsible for giving me life and allowing me to give life to future generations represented by my children and someday, their children. Like many other children of survivors, I have always felt a responsibility to achieve and give purpose to my life and teach my children how important it is to be strong, no matter what obstacles and hardships life imposes on us. In comparison to what Sali and Pesach went through, most of our problems seem rather petty.

That survival instinct that they passed on to us is the greatest gift that a parent can give a child. Sali and Pesach proved themselves to be "survivors," not only of the war, which in and of itself was an unbelievable achievement, but also after the war, going through many difficult times, but always having a positive attitude with that unbelievable will to survive whatever difficulties life presented them with.

After my mom passed away, in August 2001, at the age of 79, Pesach decided to write his book. Although I grew up with stories of the war told by my mom and her relatives and friends who also survived, it wasn't until I read Pesach's book, that I really began to understand the magnitude of what they went through during the war. Their story, as well as the stories of countless other survivors, should be told to future generations so that we never forget our roots and where we came from. Without their sacrifice, my children and I would not exist.

Now I am 62 years old. I have been married to my lovely wife, Meris, and have two wonderful children, Erica and Brandon who are 30 & 24, respectively. We have all achieved much in our lives thanks to my mom, and we will always be grateful to her for giving us the legacy of a "survivor", which teaches us that life is precious and that we must never give up because there is always hope for a better day tomorrow.

*My wife **Chava** and myself, during a visit to the U.S.,*
31 December 1999.

Amalia's birthday with her husband Shmuel,
and their children, Ophir and Yael

Celebrating family birthdays: Meris and David
with their children, Brandon and Erica